Portland Rock Climbs

A Climber's Guide
to Northwest Oregon

Revised Edition

by Tim Olson

printed by
Sheridan Books
Chelsea, MI

Cover Photo: Walter Anyan on E. Pluribus Pinhead, by Dave Sowerby.

ISBN 0-9635660-2-4
Revised Edition

Published and distributed by:
Wild Horse Adventures
Portland, Oregon

Printed by Sheridan Books
Chelsea, Michigan

Warning

The sole purpose of this guidebook is to acquaint climbers with the local crags. Rock climbing does contain certain inherent risks. Those who venture beyond this page should be thoroughly familiar with the use of modern rock equipment and techniques, and know the limits of YOUR ability. The author of this book offers *no* guarantee whatsoever about the condition of fixed gear such as bolts, pitons, or slings. This 'no guarantee' clause also includes route ratings, route descriptions, trails, etc. This guidebook is not a substitute for insight and competent instruction. As the user of this book you assume full responsibility for your own safety.

Contents

Preface

At last, the long awaited, much anticipated Portland climbers guide revision is now available. Updated for easier use, this edition will hopefully tease and entice you on to new frontiers. This version combines elements from the origional PRC while incorporating tantalizing newer climbs and climbing destinations, all in a book where secrets dare to be. Many local climbers have long desired to see this comprehensive guidebook update, yet for years a new edition of PRC was not envisioned due to unforeseen events and lack of time. But thanks to a much needed vacation period in my life, time was found and energy devoted to this revised edition which I now offer to you. Your words of encouragement have helped provide the incentive to make this new edition a reality.

Certain well-known crags like Broughton Bluff have been catapulted forward into today's limelight through a growing interest in the sport of climbing. The pulse found at the heart of this guide book is this 'latest rage' of climbing information. I hope you will benefit from this long awaited revised edition.

The Carl A. Neuberger guide **A Climber's Guide to the Columbia Gorge**, first published in 1958 in the Mazama annual was the first comprehensive guide detailing the great Gorge classics. He described pinnacles like St. Peter's Dome, Rabbit Ears, and other famous Gorge climbs—all within a compact, well written guide.

The next Oregon guidebook to put forth a compilation of climbing history and route statistics was a twice published book called **"A Climber's Guide to Oregon"** by Nicholas Dodge. Printed in 1968 and 1975 the book contains a wealth of interesting content from the earlier years of climbing and mountaineering describing many fascinating areas in Oregon from Beacon Rock to Wolf Rock.

In 1983, after years of prolific mountaineering and rock climbing, Jeff Thomas compiled and published the **"Oregon Rock"** guide. Chock full of excellent photos and descriptions, the broad scope of the guide allowed for good marketing success, while focusing needed attention on two of Portland's local crags, Broughton Bluff and Beacon Rock. A virtual avalanche of route climbing information from the 1980's quickly outpaced the guide book.

The **"Rocky Butte Quarry Guide"** published in 1987 by Robert McGown and Mike Pajunas, contributed equally toward bridging the gap in crag information, and has made a reasonable comeback via an updated edition in 1992.

In 1993 the first edition of **"Portland Rock Climbs"** took that next step to incorporate all the local rock climbing areas under one publication.

Each of the previous guidebook authors have helped immensely to focus much needed climber and community attention upon our local crags.

PRCII will primarily focus on the logistics of four crags: **Broughton Bluff, Rocky Butte, Carver Bridge Cliff** and **Beacon Rock.** On a sad note, the **Madrone Wall** has been removed from this publication due to closure of the cliff by Clackamas County over the issue of reactivating the rock quarry. Hopefully the issue will be resolved in favor of rock climbing and preservation of the cliff. The Madrone Wall is a beautiful place and is a major loss to all people.

For that special breed of climber, you will discover a comprehensive study of **Winter Ice Climbing** in the Columbia Gorge. Though this may seem an incredibly trivial sport compared to rock climbing, yet the presently available data necessitates inclusion. This sport has rapidly gained interest due to the easy access to many of the ice routes in the Gorge. Everyone, climber and hiker, should go see this staggering yet delicate wonder of the Columbia Gorge during winter ice conditions. It is spectacular, even though the season may be short. Read the chapter while gripping those ice tools.

The **Adventure Climbing** chapter offers unique destinations that will appeal to many. The section is a colorful, quality mixture of activity that encompasses a variety of challenges such as total off trail thrashing to forgotten classic pinnacles, as well as climbing at higher altitudes. Most of these places are within 150 mile radius of Portland. Read it and expand your horizons.

I'd like to thank the indispensible number of individuals who have helped toward the success of this guidebook. I am personally grateful and indebted to Nicholas Dodge, Jeff Thomas, Robert McGown and Mike Pajunas for having laid the groundwork upon which this guide is founded.

Thanks to Mark Cartier for your frankness about Beacon Rock, and to Nathan Charleton, Chad Franklin, Robert McGown, Gary Rall, Scott Tracy, Dave Sowerby, Wayne Wallace, Greg Lyon, and Steve Mrazek for freely sharing detailed first ascent particulars.

The author would like to thank R. McGown for the photos on pages 21 and 102, and also for many years of friendship. Thank you W. Wallace for the excellent action shots. In addition, I would like to thank D. Sowerby for the photo on page 45 and for the fabulous Walter Anyon cover photo, G. Murray for the Broken Rock topo, Bill Price and Jeremiah Coughlan for the photo on page 122, and Jim Apilado for the inspiring Horsetail Falls ice climbing photo.

Introduction

This second and expanded publication of the 1993 PRC guide is intended to entice avid climbers to seek a greater degree of challenge and opportunity. For right here, conveniently located in and around Portland you will find easily available rock climbing and enterprising adventures of the wildest kind. For starts, over 400 rock climbs are available to test your endurance and skill, many of which are steep, multi-pitch climbs, while other climbs are inspiring all day adventures such as the great forested walls of the Columbia River Gorge. Portland also offers the climber a great centralized location between other favorite destinations such as Smith Rock, Squamish, or City of Rocks.

Exploring has been a favorable pursuit in the Northwest since the turn of the 20th century. An upsurgence of early climbing adventures was due in part because of the building of the Columbia River Highway. Thus, recreational values of the Columbia River Gorge have become focused and persisted ever since. First came turn of the century pioneer photographers and explorer geologists of the Gorge, men like Benjamin Gifford, G. M. Weister, the Kister Brothers and Ira A. Williams who reached places that are extremely difficult to access, even today.

The next generation of adventures began to take on the serious summits and rock routes of the Gorge. Don Onthank, Lee Darling, Ray Conkling, John Ohrenschall, Carl Neuberger, Joe Leuthold, Bill Cummins, Art Maki, the Darr's, Don Comer and many others were instrumental in conquering some of the great Gorge classics. The summits they ascended are unique, tantalizing, and serious in every way, and yet are also worthy.

After the 1940's the trend gradually focused toward crags which offered easier access to practice the sport of climbing. The local crags also proved a bit more stable. The old classics of the Gorge became less and less valuable. For example: the ascents on St Peter's Dome in 1963-64 were 5 groups, 1965-68 were 3 groups, 1972 1 group, 1977 1 group, 1994 1 person! At the present rate of diminishing ascents one must wonder if anyone has reached the summit of St Peter's Dome since W. Wallace's roped solo ascent.

But the trend toward sounder rock in many ways is a great benefit, for in time these places developed into excellent crags to test skill and endurance. Thus, the present day rock climber who visits the scene comes here generally to free climb and to enjoy a comfortable outing with easy access. But has free climbing become an easy man's sport, with all its high tech gadgetry and gloss covered safety? Hardly, but in some ways it does miss the essence of raw adventure. In order to find *that* kind of adventure you will probably have to do as the early explorers did—take to the hills.

Climate and Access Information

Though the winter season can be long in Oregon virtual year-round climbing is available. One of Portlands finer climbing areas is Broughton Bluff, which faces southwest toward the winter sunshine, well protected from strong easterly winds. A definite plus when the notorious Gorge winds howl. Overall, western Oregon weather conditions are temperate. Summer months average about 80° with short peaks of 90° +, while the winters average in the 40° to 50° range. Expect heavy rain showers in November and December, March and April, which leave the crags saturated with moisture.

At **Broughton Bluff** during the spring, summer and fall, poison oak and nettles must be dealt with. Climber presence keeps most of the stinging and itching greenery pushed back, especially at the popular areas. Though summers can be muggy, it is easy to find shaded routes to climb or visit on cool overcast days. Or better still, focus your energy on other exciting areas like Beacon Rock, French's Dome, or Lamberson Butte.

Carver Bridge Cliff is a secluded small cliff of intricate beauty. The cool, perpetually shaded basalt walls have quietly 'aged' beneath dense layers of dirt and moss. The wirebrush and bolts have turned this once formidable obstacle into a challenging climbing area. Seasonally speaking, mid-April through October is prime for climbing, with comfortable mornings and perpetual shade throughout the summer months.

The great monolith of the Columbia Gorge, **Beacon Rock** (Che-che-op-tin) is situated among some of the most vivid scenery in the Pacific Northwest. Strong winds and cold temperatures keep Beacon nearly void of climber traffic in the winter, even though sporadic climbing days do exist.

The best months to climb here are mid-April through September, but do be aware that *all* of the south face is *closed* from February 1 until approximately July 15 due to Peregrine Falcon nesting. Check with the state park manager for further updated information.

Beacon Rock offers steep, highly sustained, full and multi-pitch, technically demanding climbs at all levels of difficulty. This *is* bold climbing! Beacon's easiest route is 5.7 and multi-pitch, while the majority of routes range from 5.10 to 5.11+. To date the most difficult climbs established are 5.12+ with virtually unlimited potential beyond that, whether free or nailing.

The climbing routes are of the highest standard, easily taking first place locally in bold, technical rock climbs. Many of the dihedral systems were nailed in the 1960's and 70's. Later, these nailing routes were free climbed at surprisingly moderate ratings, thus establishing some of the finest stemming and jamming problems in the region. All great reasons to visit this monolith of the Columbia River Gorge.

Rocky Butte Quarry is a unique crag located in northeast Portland near the conjunction of I-205 and I-84. This easily accessible crag is a great place to top-rope or to learn the sport. As the name implies, the place was a rock quarry prior to 1956, but now the trees shade the crags in a canopy of cool comfortable shade, great for summer climbing. Of those early climbers who visited this north-facing crag during the 1960's and 70's to practice their free and aid climbing skills, only a few known ascents remain from that period. It was not until mid to late 1980's when the crag was thoroughly explored for climber use. Video Bluff, Toothpick Wall and Breakfast Cracks have become favorite areas to climb at on a hot summer afternoon. If you can overlook the rough outer appearance, the broken glass, spraypaint, and litter, then you will begin to see the inner beauty of this favorite haunt.

Climbing Classifications

The Yosemite Decimal System (YDS) is the standard method for rating the difficulty of climbs in Oregon as well as across the U.S. This system is subdivided into three sections: **Overall Difficulty** (Grade), **Free Climbing Difficulty** (Class), and **Aid Difficulty**.

For the longer routes an **Overall Difficulty** rating (Roman numerals I through VI) denotes how long it will take an average party. For example: a Grade I in a few hous, Grade II in a half day, Grade III in most of a day. A Grade IV one long hard day where the hardest pitch is no less than 5.7, Grade V in one long day if the climbers are experienced and fast, otherwise 1 1/2 days+ should be expected while the hardest pitch is usually at least 5.8, Grade VI requires multiple days to ascend and often includes mixed free climbing and nailing. It is purely subjective, though. Some climbers may be able to climb very efficiently on two Grade IV routes while others may barely manage a Grade II without bivouacking. Most of the climbs within this guide fall between the Grades I and III.

Free Climbing Difficulty, or technical free climbing, is rated on an ascending scale from 5.0 to 5.14. This open-ended scale allows for future routes of increasing difficulty. If a particular pitch contains a series of moves of the same difficulty, a higher rating is usually assigned. Further subgrading separates the "easier" 5.10's from the "harder" 5.10's by using the letters A,B,C and D. Some free-climbing routes at the local crags are underrated due to toproping before leading. The best solution is to rate the climb according to an on-sight or "flash" lead by a person unfamiliar with the route in question.

The art of modern nailing, **Aid Climbing Difficulty**, is quite unlike its neighbor mentioned in the paragraph above. Both the technical severity of the piton placement, and the climber's security are linked to the same rating. In the sport of nailing, the letter A indicates aid climbing, while the number 0 through 6 (and higher) indicates the degree of nailing.

A-0 pendulum, shoulder stand, tension rest or a quick move up by pulling on protection.

A-1 placements still hold charging rhinos.

A-2 is more difficult to place but offers some good protection.

A-3 involves marginal placements and the potential for a short fall.

A-4 has frequent marginal pro and will only hold body weight.

A-5 entails enough marginal pro to risk a good 50-60 foot fall.

A-6 involves full pitch leads of A-4 and ground fall "zipper" potential.

Modern nailing equipment has profoundly changed the way in which climber's approach a prospective route. Knifeblades, RURP's, Bird Beaks,

Peckerheads, and a variety of hooks offer new ways to aid climb at the extreme edge. Since free climbs are often maintained as free climbs certainly some nailing routes should be maintained as nailing routes.

For those routes requiring a "seriousness" rating, they are as follows:

R: Serious fall potential; may involve questionable or poor protection; serious injury is likely.

X: Ground fall potential; very poor to no protection available; serious or fatal injury possible.

Beware that the seriousness ratings in this guidebook are not the final word concerning a route's extreme nature. All routes in this guide are subject to seriousness and may be inherently dangerous. Proceed with caution and climb at your own risk!

The "Star" or **Quality** rating used throughout this book is designed to allow climbers to selectively choose the interesting or more aesthetic climbs. This is a highly subjective system, for many of the unstarred routes are worthy of attention, while some routes truly deserve dust and obscurity.

No Stars: Average quality route.

One Star (★): Good quality route, recommended.

Two Stars (★★): Excellent route, good position, quality climbing, sound rock, highly recommended.

Three Stars (★★★): Highest quality, should not be missed in a lifetime!

Of these starred routes not all will be bolted face climbs. Some will be crack climbs, several will be short but worthy, a few will be two routes connected together to create a finer quality climb. And yes, some of the starred routes will be multi-pitch 5.9 crack climbs.

To bring the quality rating closer to home, the author will *not* be comparing the "star" routes of one crag to another. Specifically, the quality climbs at Broughton will vary from the quality routes at Beacon Rock or Smith Rock. Thus, when

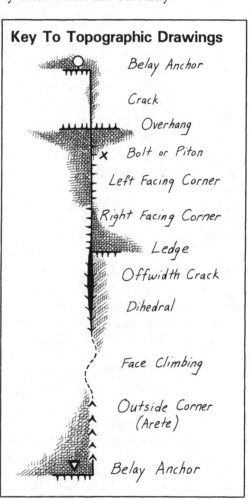

Key To Topographic Drawings

Belay Anchor

Crack

Overhang

Bolt or Piton

Left Facing Corner

Right Facing Corner

Ledge

Offwidth Crack

Dihedral

Face Climbing

Outside Corner (Arete)

Belay Anchor

4

visiting a particular crag the "star" will represent the more favorable, interesting routes at that cliff only. The following chart shows the relative relationship between four international ratings.

INTERNATIONAL GRADE SCALE

YDS	UIAA	Australian	French
5.3	IV	11	2
5.4	IV+	12	3
5.5	V-	12 / 13	4a
5.6	V	13 / 14	4b
5.7	V+	15-17	4c
5.8	VI-	18	5a
5.9	VI	19	5b
5.10a	VI+	20	5c
5.10b	VII-	20	6a
5.10c	VII	21	6a+
5.10d		21	6b
5.11a	VI+	22	6b+
5.11b	VIII-	22	6c
5.11c	VIII	23	6c+
5.11d	VIII+	24	7a
5.12a	IX-	25	7a+
5.12b	IX	26	7b
5.12c	IX+	27	7b+
5.12d		27	7c
5.13a		28	7c+
5.13b	X-	29	8a
5.13c		30	8a+
5.13d		31	8b
5.14a		32	8b+
5.14b		?	8c
5.14c		?	8c+

Technical Equipment

Innovative, and effective improvements in rock climbing equipment over the last 20 years has produced ground breaking results for the sport. Friends, TCU's, RP's, curved Stoppers, bolts, and tailored rock shoes have contributed greatly to the overall enjoyment of climbing. Depending on your destination a rack of something slightly more than QD's would be an excellent start. The following is a rack of excess luggage, and from this you can generally determine your needs per climb.

QD's, small to large wired stoppers (1/8" to 1 1/2"), camming devices like

TCU's (1/2" to 1 1/2"), or Friends (1" to 4"), runners, and Hexcentrics, or Big Bro, if a particularly *fine* off-width crack suits your fancy. Specialized pro like RP's, or Steel Nuts may be necessary on a few desperate routes. You can angle toward a rather lean rack of the above gear when visiting Carver Bridge Cliff, while a more comprehensive rack would prepare you for Beacon Rock.

For those interested in pursuing a career in nailing, a number of outrageous routes are available at all the local crags. Consider the following to assist you in your climb: Knifeblades, Hooks, RURP's, bashies, tie-off loops, etc.

For the climbing enthusiast who wishes to be informed as to the latest in gear many sources are available that offer competitive prices: REI, OMC, Mountain Shop, Next Adventure, Climb Max, mail order magazines, and the Internet. Check the Yellow Pages, and talk with friends to find other sources where you can purchase new or used equipment.

Styles and Ethics

Contemporary climbing views consist of two forces: style and ethics. Style is how you climb on the rock while ethics are what you do to the rock. Present trends such as top-roping, rappel inspection, pre-protection and free-soloing are styles. Bolting, chiseling holds, gardening or scarring the rock is an ethic. Remember, ethics are not permanent law but merely presently accepted cohesive ideas. An absolute standard *never* changes. By reading any climbing history book we can be rest assured that style and ethics have been shaped and molded over the years.

Presently accepted trends such as route cleaning, bolting, and pre-inspection are generally accepted ideas at most crags. Refrain from the use of modular holds. Do not place new rappel anchors or more fixed gear on established routes. Any route, whether established via free or nailing should be considered as such; it is the first ascentionists present choice. Chiseling is not recommended. People will continue to climb at increasingly higher standards in the years to come.

The roto-powered drill has transformed the sport of route development, yet restraint should be exercised in bolting. Every route does not need bolts. The power drill of this era may be the scourge of future generations.

There are individuals with strong egocentric ideals who attempt to dominate their personal climbing area with a covert fist policy, usually based upon threats and action. This is neither style nor ethics, yet it does occur at places such as Beacon Rock, Broughton Bluff, and even at the Menegerie. Be aware that some routes that you may wish to climb may not be available as a lead route due to missing gear.

Ongoing community involvement in caring for the crags by all of us will help keep these places available in the years to come. Enjoy the sport of rock climbing for its social and outdoor benefits by respecting everyone as well as the rock.

Wayne Wallace leading Crash of the Titans (5.10C)

Broughton Bluff

Broughton Bluff is the all-time original Portland crag. Approached by a few sturdy rock climbers who began to utilize this crag in the late 1950's the popularity of this crag has continued to grow to this day. This dark, moss-covered basalt bluff has yielded many time-honored classics which the modern rock climber will find enjoyable.

Located along the eastern outskirts of Portland, Broughton offers easy access and an extensive selection of secluded 160' high walls on State Park land. The crag is an excellent year-round climbing park. Individuals from all walks of life come here to learn the ropes of climbing, to build courage, as well as to test their limits.

The early ascents were completed using ground-up mixed aid and free climbing. One of the first to become established was the **Hanging Gardens** (5.10 A) route ascended by Bob Waring, John Wells, and Bruce Holcomb in 1965. Today it is considered a trade route classic. This climb stands as an honorable testament to those early days of exploratory aid climbing.

Perhaps the finest achievement at Broughton took place in 1968 when Steve Strauch and Jim O'Connell ascended the North Face by the super classic and ever popular **Gandalf's Grip** (5.9+). This route is one of the best crack climbs of this rating at Broughton Bluff.

The 1970's heralded forth a small but active core of climbers who succeeded to establish many more routes. Jim Mayers, Gail Van Hoorn, Alan Campbell, Dave Jensen, Talbot Bielefeldt, Dean Fry and others opened the doors by aid climbing routes like **Peach Cling** (5.11 B), **Mr. Potato** (5. 11 A) and **Sesame Street** (5.9+), all of which were ascended in 1972; **Peer Pressure** (5.10 D) in 1973, **Face Not Friction** (5.11 D) in 1975 as well as **Classic Crack** (early 1970's).

The mid-1970's brought a subtle change as rock climbers pushed beyond the known standards, firmly establishing a whole new dimension of free climbing. Many of the older routes were ascended free without the use of direct aid. Even the new climbs were pushed beyond the 5.9 standard.

Red Eye (5.10 C) and **Sheer Stress** (5.10 A) were done in 1976; **Sandy's Direct** (5.10 C) and **Physical Graffiti** (5.10 D), a short, nasty roof problem, were put up in 1977. Beyond the Red Wall stands the superb cliff known as the Bat Wall, where **Superstition** (5.11 A) and **Hanging Tree** (5.10 D) broke new barriers in 1977 as well. It was this massive and secluded wall that became the key to the next generation.

The climbers who were instrumental in the 1970's are Doug Bower, Monty Mayko, Bruce Casey, Robert McGown, Mike Smelser, Jeff Thomas, Ken Currens, Mark Cartier, Jay Kerr, Dan Foote and others. They focused their energy towards free climbing the untapped routes of their time.

Afterward, nearly ten silent years descended upon Broughton Bluff. The summer of 1990, brought another breed of climbers who noticed a realm of blank space still to be touched. The powered roto-hammer quickly unraveled the final mysteries of Broughton, bringing the 5.12 rating to the crag.

The **Unnamed Aid Route** on the Bat Wall, after numerous free climbing attempts, was finally overcome. A name with real bite stood out: **Dracula** (5.12 A). A virtually endless series of climbs soon followed, some more precious than the richest diamond mines of Africa. **Bela Lugosi** (5.12 C), **Bad Omen** (5.12 B), and **Kashmir** (5.12 B) were all established in 1990. In 1991, **Heart of Darkness** (5.12 B) brought renewed interest to the Jungle Cliff, while **Bloodline** (5.12 B) continued the legacy in 1992 at the Bat Wall.

Gary Rall, Wayne Wallace, Dave Sowerby, Jay Green and many others have helped to push the standards of the nineties. The mysteries of Broughton met a new destiny.

Broughton Bluff is composed of 13 major and distinct walls, with six minor subcliffs scattered in between. Of the 13 larger cliffs, ten will be detailed with topo maps. For these are the ones which contain the vast majority of established and accessible climbs. The others (such as Aerie, Perihelion and Eclipse Wall) are located on private land and are not available. The ten are as follows, from left to right: the North Face, Hanging Gardens Wall, Red Wall, Bridge Cliff, Spring Rock, Bat Wall, the tiny subcliff called Broken Rock, Trinity Wall, Berlin Wall, Jungle Cliff and New Frontier Cliff.

Broughton Bluff is located off I-84 at the Lewis & Clark State Park exit east of Troutdale. Turn south at the T-intersection, drive beneath the railroad tracks and park in the State Park day use area. Walk south to the steep hillside and follow the climbers path that leads upward. Either take the path straight up to where it meets rock or follow the graded path that angles up right to the Hanging Gardens Wall and Red Wall. The general line of descent for the North Face and Hanging Gardens Wall is down the third class ridge between these two walls.

Broughton Bluff

North Face

1. **Traffic Court** 5.9 ★
   60' Thin Pro to 2" TCU's suggested
   Start as for Gandalf's left variation and climb past a bolt to a stance. Ascend a vertical corner (piton) till it eases to a slab. Muscle over a final bulge directly above then step right to rejoin with Gandalf's Grip at the belay.

2. **G.G. Variation** 5.9+
   Pro to 1 1/2"
   Start up left from the cave past a bolt to a small ledge. Continue up the

North Face Wall

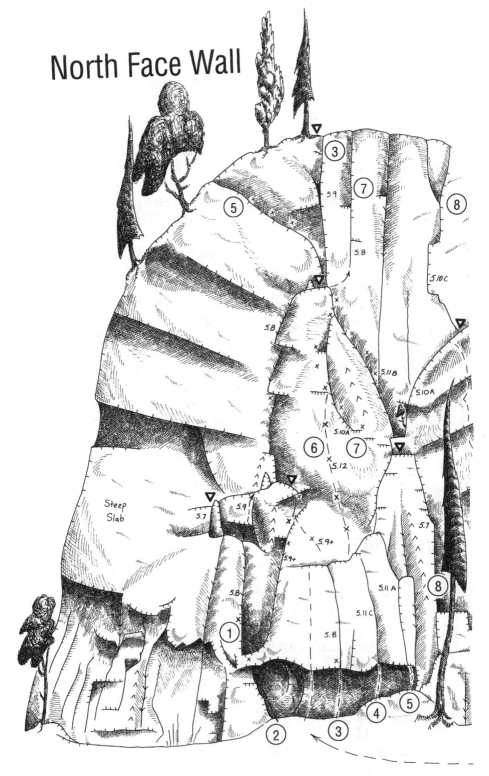

5.9

5.8

5.8

5.8

Steep
Slab

5.7

5.9

5.7

5.9+

5.9+

5.8

5.11B

5.10A

5.10A

5.12

5.11A

5.11C

5.8

5.10C

5.7

5.11A

5.11C

③ ⑦ ⑧ ⑤ ⑥ ⑦ ① ② ③ ④ ⑤ ⑧

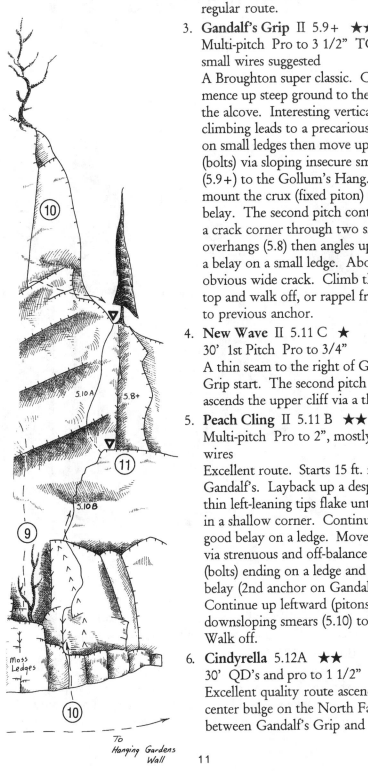

right leaning dihedral to rejoin the regular route.

3. **Gandalf's Grip** II 5.9+ ★★★
Multi-pitch Pro to 3 1/2" TCU's or small wires suggested
A Broughton super classic. Commence up steep ground to the right of the alcove. Interesting vertical crack climbing leads to a precarious stance on small ledges then move up left (bolts) via sloping insecure smears (5.9+) to the Gollum's Hang. Surmount the crux (fixed piton) and belay. The second pitch continues up a crack corner through two small overhangs (5.8) then angles up right to a belay on a small ledge. Above is an obvious wide crack. Climb this to the top and walk off, or rappel from here to previous anchor.

4. **New Wave** II 5.11 C ★
30' 1st Pitch Pro to 3/4"
A thin seam to the right of Gandalf's Grip start. The second pitch is A2 and ascends the upper cliff via a thin crack.

5. **Peach Cling** II 5.11 B ★★
Multi-pitch Pro to 2", mostly small wires
Excellent route. Starts 15 ft. right of Gandalf's. Layback up a desperate thin left-leaning tips flake until it ends in a shallow corner. Continue up to a good belay on a ledge. Move up left via strenuous and off-balance moves (bolts) ending on a ledge and bolt belay (2nd anchor on Gandalf's). Continue up leftward (pitons) on downsloping smears (5.10) to the top. Walk off.

6. **Cindyrella** 5.12A ★★
30' QD's and pro to 1 1/2"
Excellent quality route ascending the center bulge on the North Face between Gandalf's Grip and Peach

Hanging Gardens Wall
-Left Half

Cling. Joins with Risky Business. Either rappel from Gandalf's second belay anchor with two ropes or climb up and then walk off.

7. **Risky Business** 5.10 A (R) ★★
40'   QD's and pro to 1" Cams recommended.
Start at the first belay on Peach Cling. Step left onto a sloping series of ledges (crux) passing several bolts. Continue up good holds until able to join with Peach Cling then to the belay anchor on Gandalf's Grip. A

surprisingly quality climb of only moderate difficulty. The final pitch turns right and around a spectacular corner to a hidden jug, then ascends a crack dihedral leading to the summit.

8. **Reckless Driver** II 5.10 C ★
Multi-Pitch   Pro to 3" Cams or TCU's helpful
A good climb with variety and little traffic. Start 5 ft. right of Peach Cling. Move up an easy corner to a ledge then up a right-facing corner (5.6) then

13

leftward to the Peach Cling belay. Up to the right is a bush. Thrash over the bush past a crux (5.10 A) up an easy right angling ramp system to a belay anchor. Exit off down right to a large fir tree (rappel) or from the top of the ramp, step left then climb up a thin crack system (5.10 C) to the summit.

9. _____

10. **Sweet Emotion** II 5.10 B
    165' Pro to 2 1/2" Needs bolts on 2nd pitch
    Unusual route on tricky pro. A little hard to locate.

11. **American Graffiti** 5.8+
    30' Pro to 2"
    Climb the crack just below the large fir tree on the west edge of the North Face.

Hanging Gardens Wall - Left Half

1. **Giant's Staircase** 5.6

2. **Edges and Ledges** 5.8 ★★★
   60' 4 QD's and pro to 2"
   Start right of G.S. Climb up a corner to a large ledge, then embark up the bolted face above.

3. **The Sickle** 5.8 ★★★
   60' Pro to 4"
   This popular climb is the obvious curving offwidth 30 ft. up the wall.
   This area of blocky ledges and numerous cracks is an excellent top-rope area.

4. **The Hammer** 5.7 ★
   60' Pro to 3"

5. **Prometheus Slab** 5.4
   60' Pro to 3"
   An original 1960's climb. Ascend an easy corner near a tree to a ledge then up right via a wide groove.

6. **Spud** 5.9
   60' Pro to 3"

7. **Tip City** 5.10 A ★★
   40' Pro to 1 1/2"
   An excellent thin crack. Locate two parallel cracks that join with Chockstone Chimney at a ledge. The left route is Tip City.

8. **Lean Years** 5.10 C ★
   40' Pro to 1 1/2"
   The right parallel crack. Both routes make excellent options to practice thin crack climbing.

9. **Hangover** 5.11

40' (TR)

10. **Chockstone Chimney** 5.9
    80' Pro to 4"
    An original 1960's climb.

11. **Milestone** 5.7
    80' Pro to 3"

Hanging Gardens Wall - Right Half

12. **Loose Block Overhang** 5.9 ★★★
    120' Pro to 2 1/2"
    This very popular climb offers three optional starting points. You may
    climb a corner to an offwidth (5.9) 25 ft. to the top of a large block. Bolt
    anchor. Or climb on the left via steep steps (5.8) and an offwidth move to
    the same anchor. Or, on the right ascend steep columns to a ledge then
    step up left via a short jam crack and left to the anchor. On the 2nd pitch,
    jam up a slightly overhung crack (crux) until it eases onto a ledge and bolt
    belay. Maneuver up a 5.8 left-facing corner, swing right onto a slab (piton)
    then up an easy blocky section and walk off left. Or from the belay exit
    up a left slanting crack (20') on steep rock and thin holds.

13. **Grace and Danger** 5.11 B (R)
    15' Pro to 1 1/2" Cams recommended
    Ascend the outside arete next to the 1st pitch of Loose Block.

14. **Slapfest** 5.12 B ★★
    40'   6 QD's and minor pro to 1"
    Climb the superb bolted face immediately right of Loose Block. A rather
    stiff, unusual route. Joins with Least Resistance.

15. **Least Resistance** 5.10 A
    30' Pro to 1"
    Start as for Hanging Gardens but step up left of the maple tree to ascend
    the left-leaning seam (bolts). Turn an outside corner and up to the bolt
    anchor on Loose Block.

16. **Dynamic Resistance** 5.10 D ★★
    80' QD's and Pro to 1 1/2"
    Climb a strenuous dihedral between Least Resistance and Sandy's Direct.
    Excellent climb.

17. **Sandy's Direct** 5.10 C ★★
    120' Pro to 2" including small wires
    An exciting route and a must for everyone. Start as for Hanging Gardens
    route (stay left of the maple tree belay) but go straight up the vertical
    corner system 60 ft. to blocky ledges then exit left to walk off.

18. **Face Not Friction** 5.11 D ★★
    60' QD's and minor pro to start
    Quality climbing, worth the effort. Up and left of the maple tree belay is

Hanging Gardens Wall
- Right Half

Blocky and Loose
No Routes

5.11 A

28

5.8

12

5.8

5.10 C

11

5.11 D

5.10 C

16

18

5.7

5.9

5.10 A

15

17

Poison
Oak

Steep
Slab

5.7

5.9

5.12 B

13

5.8

14

5.9

5.9

5.11 B

5.6

5.6

12

19

16

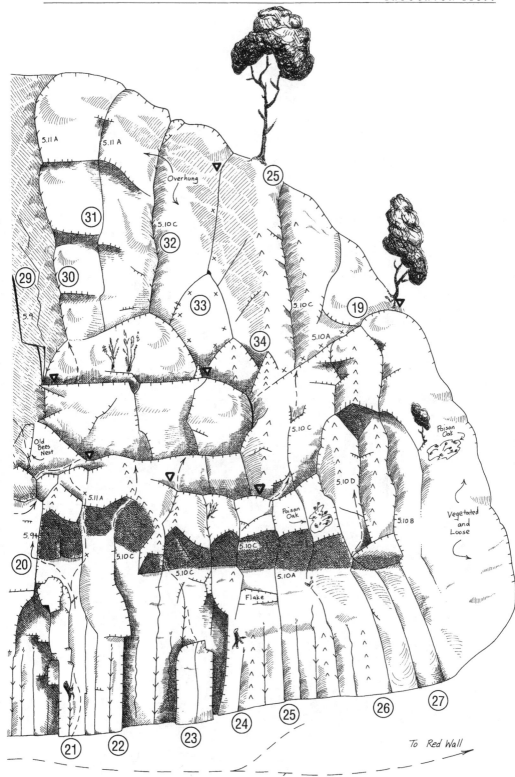

5.11 A

5.11 A

Overhung

5.10 C

㉛

㉜

㉙

㉚

5.9

㉝

㉞

5.10 C

⑲

5.10 A

5.10 C

Old
Bees
Nest

5.11 A

5.9+

Poison
Oak

5.10 D

Poison
Oak

5.10 B

Vegetated
and
Loose

⑳

5.10 C

5.10 C

5.10 C

5.10 C

Poison
Oak

5.10 A

Flake

㉑

㉒

㉓

㉔

㉕

㉖

㉗

To Red Wall

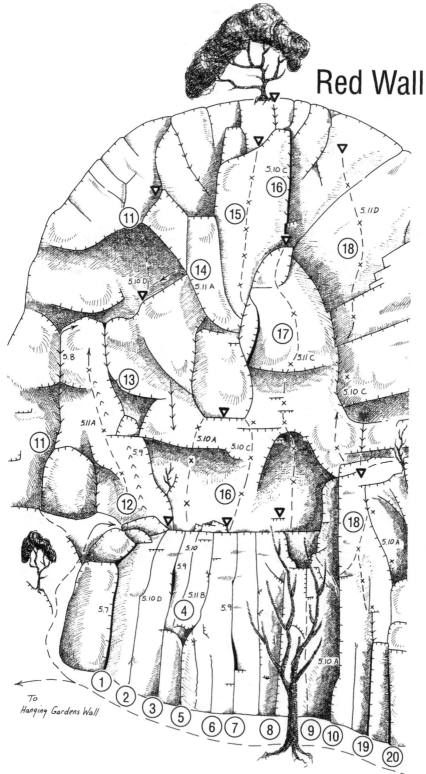

Red Wall

To
Hanging Gardens Wall

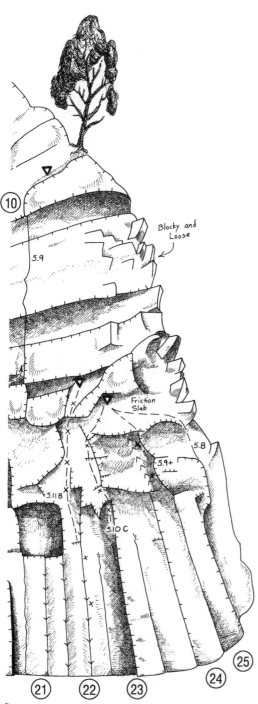

Blocky and Loose

5.9

Friction Slab

5.8

5.9+

5.11 B

5.10 C

(21) (22) (23) (24) (25)

(10)

a partially fixed face-seam problem on vertical rock. Climb this to a bolt anchor at a small ledge. Rappel or continue up left via steep, bushy cracks to an upper ledge, then exit left to hike down.

19. **Hanging Gardens** II 5.10 A (or 5.6 A0) ★★★
Multi-pitch   Pro to 1 1/2"
One of the original Broughton favorites put up in 1965. Begins via numerous starts which lead up to the maple tree. Belay anchor. From the tree move right 10 ft. across a slab, pull over a bulge, then right to an anchor for Mr. Potato. Traverse rightward along ledges then up a short corner and bolt belay on the left. Move back right and around a blind corner. Free (5.10 A) or A0 (fixed pitons) diagonally right 20 ft. along the "bicycle path" to grassy ledges and an oak tree belay. Walk off.

20. **B.F.D.** 5.9+
30'   Pro to 1"
Harder now that the flake is gone.

The following 5 routes have belay anchors at about 40 ft. up.

21. **Mr. Potato** 5.11 A
40'   Pro to 3/4"
Unusual yet interesting climb. Start same as B.F.D., but continue directly up a right facing near vertical corner. Pull over several bulges to join with Hanging Gardens. Rappel.

22. **From Something to Nothing** 5.10 C
40'   Pro to 1" and QD's
A good corner problem immediately right of Mr. Potato. Climb

To Bridge Cliff

up a corner until you can exit up right to join Hanging Gardens.

23. **Fun in the Mud** 5.10 C
40' Pro to 1" and QD's

24. **Circus Act** 5.10 C
40' Pro to 1" including TCU's

25. **Shining Star** 5.10 A ★
140' Pro to 2"
A great first pitch. Located on the right side of Hanging Gardens Wall.
Climb a crack on a mossy slab immediately right of a maple tree. Pull
through the bulge (5.10 A) and continue up to an easy stance on sloping
ledges. Step left to join Hanging Gardens route or step right and climb a
broken crack system (5.10 C) via edges and corners. Joins H. G. route at
the "bicycle path".

26. **Hung Jury** 5.10 D
130' Pro to 2 1/2" including pitons

27. **Hang 'Em High** 5.10 B
130' Pro to 2"

The following 7 routes are located in a small amphitheatre above the
second pitch of the Hanging Gardens route.

28. **Main Vein** 5.11 B
30' Pro to 2"
This is the obvious prow right of Face Not Friction and above the maple
tree belay. Follow the standard Hanging Gardens route past the tree, but
at the old bees nest move up left around the corner by way of a crack.
Once on the steep slab angle left then right and finish up a bolted arete
until it joins with Sesame Street.

29. **Sesame Street** 5.9+ ★★
Pro to 3"
Excellent but short. Climb the first pitch of Hanging Gardens. At the
piton anchor for Mr. Potato step up left on easy ledges to a bolt belay. To
your left is a slightly overhung zigzag jam crack. Climb this 15 ft. to
another belay. Rappel with two ropes or traverse left along ledges to the
descent trail.

30. **Demian** 5.10 D ★★
30' Pro to 3" TCU's optional
Superb, strenuous route ascending a desperate overhanging crack.

31. **Endless Sleep** 5.11 A (R)
30' Pro to 2"

32. **Peer Pressure** 5.10 C (R)
30' Pro to 2'
Poorly protected at the start but exciting stemming above. From the bolt

anchor at the base of Scorpion Seams angle up left on slabs then ascend the overhung corner (pitons) to the top.

33. **Scorpion Seams** 5.12 C/D ★★
30' 6 QD's
On the right face of the overhanging alcove is a bolted series of seams. The left start is 5.12 C but both starts lead to the same anchor.

34. **Black Prow** 5.12 A
30' Pro to 2"

Red Wall

1. **Arch de Triumph** 5.7
20' Pro to 4"

2. **Arcturus** 5.10 D
20' (TR)

3. **Anastasia** 5.9
25' (TR)
Climb a thin crack to a flared crux problem.

4. **Dry Bones** 5.10+ ★★
25' (TR)

5. **On the Loose** 5.11 A ★★
30' (TR)
An excellent top-rope problem left of Classic Crack

6. _____ 5.13
30' (TR)

7. **Classic Crack** 5.9+
★★★
30' Pro to 2"
That's exactly what it is. A beautiful jam crack that splits a smooth wall. Can be top-roped by scrambling up an access trail to the left.

8. **Thai Stick** 5.10 D
★★
30' QD's

9. **Mr. Bentley** 5.11+
★★
30' (TR)
Remarkable route; physically exciting.

Robert McGown leading the roof on Physical Graffiti (5.10D)

21

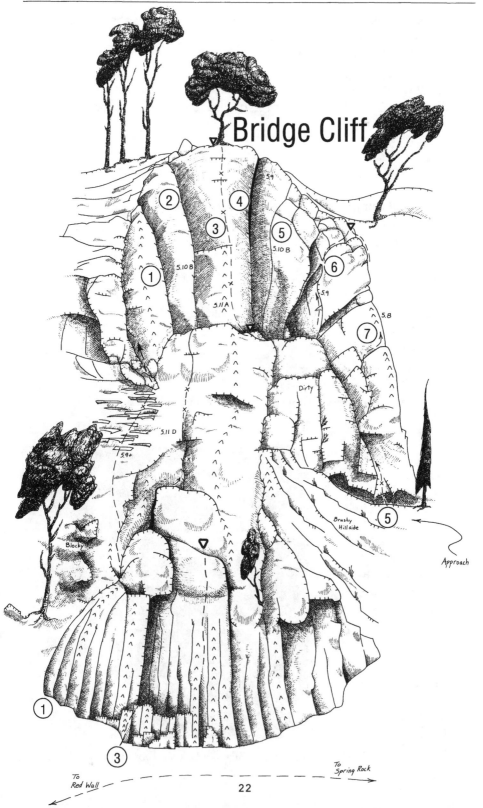

Bridge Cliff

10. **Sheer Stress** II 5.10 A ★★★
Multi-pitch   Pro to 2 1/2"
Very popular, quality route. One of the ten super classics. Commence up
the shalow left-facing corner (crux) 15 ft. right of Classic Crack. Climb up
until it eases then turn an odd corner right to an anchor. Belay. Move
right to a semi-detached block (maple tree) then climb straight up the hand
crack (5.9+) until possible to exit right on good holds to a ledge. Rappel
with 2 ropes from bolt anchor.

The following routes are located generally above Classic Crack or Sheer
Stress and can be accessed by most of the previous routes on the Red Wall.

11. **Physical Graffiti** II 5.10 D ★★★
Multi-pitch   Pro to 2"
A fascinating route highlighted by a hand jam roof problem. Move up an
easy dihedral (5.7) on the left corner of Red Wall and above Arch De
Triumph. Upon
reaching a roof traverse
right to a ledge and bolt
belay. Jam the over-
hang! The climb eases
onto a steep crack and
an anchor. Rappel or
finish up one of the
upper variations (5.10 A
and dirty).

12. **Habitual Ritual**
5.11 A
30'   4 QD's and minor
pro to 2"

13. **Physical Direct** 5.9
30'   Pro to 2" TCU's
recommended

14. **Hit the Highway**
5.11 A ★
30'   Pro to 1 1/2"
Good yet surprisingly
hard lead. Begin on the
ledges next to the maple
tree. Ascend directly up
a steep bolted face (5.10
A) then move right to
the Red Eye belay. Step
right and up (5.10 A) a

Heather Macdonald on Sheer Stress (5.10 A)

few moves until possible to move left to an ominous looking steep corner. Climb this and exit left to join with Physical Graffiti or jam directly up a vertical crack to a ledge. Angle up left to a bolt belay. Rappel.

15. **Kashmir** 5.12 A ★★★
    40' 5 QD's and minor pro to 2 1/2" (#5 Rock and 2 1/2" Friend)
    This superb line is located on the brilliant orange face in the upper amphitheatre. Ascend Red Eye approximately 30 ft. until possible to enter onto a steep bolted face on the left. Rappel from bolt anchors with 2 ropes unless you rappel to the Red Eye anchor.

16. **Red Eye** II 5.10 C ★★
    Multi-Pitch   Pro to 2 1/2" (1st pitch is 4 QD's)
    A very popular route, especially the first pitch. Lead Classic Crack or start at the ledge above Classic, and climb a bolted face past a round red "eye" to a bolt anchor on a ledge to your left. Belay, then step right and up a crack system to easier ground. Belay at stance. Finish up a wide offwidth corner (5.10C) with numerous edges. Exit left then up to the tree. Rappel with 2 ropes or walk off.

17. **Critical Mass** 5.11 C ★★★
    80' 8 QD's and optional pro to 1 1/2"
    Impressive bolted climb on a vertical orange wall. Retrobolting in 1991 focused the route from a 5.11 A problem to a 5.11 C face. Ascend Sheer Stress for 30', step left and then up the steep wall above. The bulge is the crux. Joins with Red Eye at a bolt anchor below the prominent offwidth.

18. **E. Pluribus Pinhead** (a.k.a. Pinhead) 5.11 D ★★★
    100' 8 QD's and minor pro to 1 1/2"
    A fabulous route ascending the beautiful upper orange face of the Red Wall. Commence up approximately 18 ft. of Sheer Stress, step right via jugs and a shaky mantle then up to a bolt anchor. Move up left (bolts) then up an easy corner and finally up right onto a desperate vertical face to a bolt anchor. Rappel with 2 ropes unless descending to a nearby anchor.

19. **Opus** 5.11+ (R)
    25' 3 QD's to 1st anchor

    The next several routes are just to the right of Sheer Stress on a darker shaded section of wall.

20. **Sheer Energy** 5.10 A ★
    45' Pro to 1 1/2"
    Step to the top of several free-standing columns of basalt, then climb a crack up a short face (bolts) to a belay anchor.

21. _____

22. **Hard Body** 5.11 B ★★★
    50' 6 QD's

Very popular route. Unusual crux. Commence up a shallow corner to a strenuous move then pull through a bulge and up steep rock to an anchor capped by a roof. Rappel.

23. **Shoot from the Hip** 5.10 C ★★
    45' Pro to 1" and QD's
    Fun climb with big holds and a crack to start.

24. **No Friction** 5.9+
    45' Pro and QD's

25. **That's the Way** 5.8
    45' Pro ?

Bridge Cliff

1. **Under Your Belt** 5.9+ (R)
   165' Pro to 2"
   A little known climb ascending the blocky 5th class section on the lower left. From a belay ledge 2/3 up the wall, step left and finish up a clean dihedral to the top. Rappel or walk off.

2. **Walk on the Wild Side**
   5.10 C/D ★★
   45' Pro to 2"
   The standard approach to this classic begins via the first pitch of Fruit Bat. Belay on the halfway ledge, then traverse left roughly 15 ft. past a central corner (Spidermonkey) to a second left-leaning corner. Ascend this to the top. Rappel or walk off.

3. **Edge of Eternity** II 5.11 C ★
   Multi-pitch Pro to 2"
   A long climb that begins on the lower section of wall. Climb the dihedral and move right around a difficult corner (5.11) to dirty ledges. Above an easy wide corner is a clean angular face with bolts. Climb this (crux) to a big ledge. Belay. Step right and climb (bolts and pitons) the right face of an arete (5.10 A) to a tiny ledge, then a short face to the tree belay. Rappel or walk off.

4. **Spidermonkey** 5.9 ★
   40' Pro to 3"
   This is the large, dark dihedral on the upper face above the belay ledge.

5. **Fruit Bat** II 5.10 B ★
   Multi-pitch Pro to 2"
   This is the best option for approaching all the upper tier routes. Start past a bolt into a sloping corner. Exit up left via grassy ledges and corners to a ledge. Belay here. On the right face of the deep dihedral is a thin finger crack. Ascend this and top out. Note: several of the previous routes have original start points but are heavily vegetated and dirty.

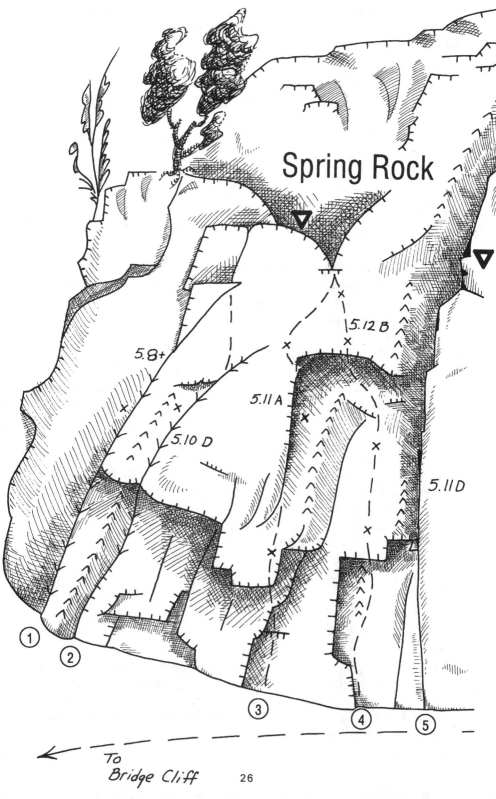

Spring Rock

5.8+

5.12 B

5.11 A

5.10 D

5.11 D

① ② ③ ④ ⑤

To
Bridge Cliff   26

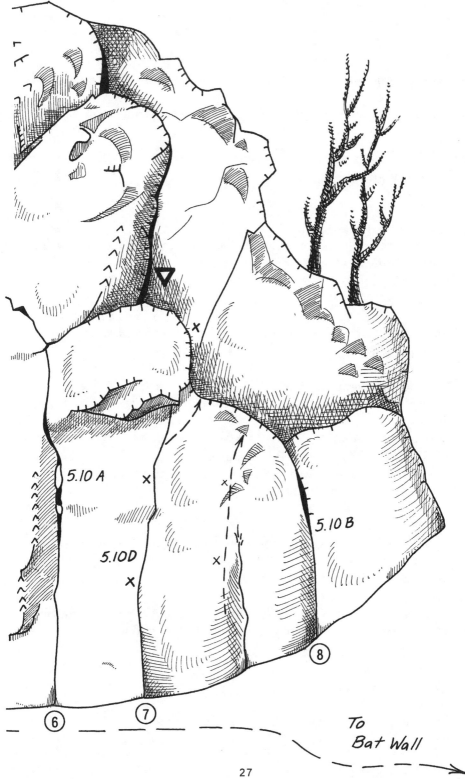

5.10 A

5.10 D

5.10 B

⑥   ⑦   ⑧

To
Bat Wall

6. **Seventh Sojourn** 5.9
   Pro unknown
7. **Shandor** 5.9
   Pro to 3"
⊗. **Eagle's Wing** 5.12 A
   Pro QD's
   Climbs the face to the right of the start of Edge of Eternity.

Spring Rock

1. **Toe Cleavage** 5.8+
   30' Pro to 1"
2. **Velcro Fly** 5.10 D
   30' QD's and minor pro to 1"
   Located on the left side. The route is highlighted by a thin crux move in a shallow corner at a bulge. Wander up easier slabs to a bolt belay.
3. **Free Bird** 5.11 A ★★
   40' Pro to 1"
   Excellent route. Step up to a small corner, reach left, then climb a second corner to a roof. Exit left onto slabs that lead up left to a bolt anchor.
4. **Ground Effects** 5.12 A/B ★★
   40' 4 QD's
   Probably the most unusual and fascinating route on Spring Rock. The climb involves two roof moves using very unorthodox technique. Solve the puzzle.
5. **Jumping Jack Thrash** 5.11 D (R) ★★
   40' Pro to 1" TCU's and RP's recommended
   A great classic climb. Ascend a thin crack in the center of the face to a bolt anchor under an overhang. Rappel.
6. **The Spring** 5.10A/B ★
   40' Pro to 2"
   This interesting flared crack joins at the Jumping Jack Thrash anchor. Rappel.
7. **Short Fuse** 5.10 C ★★
   35' 3 QD's
   Yes, it is quite short, but it is still a worthy climb. Ascend the blank face and exit right to a ledge, step up left to a bolt anchor. Rappel.
8. **Dyno-mite** 5.10 B
   35' Pro to 1 1/2"
⊗. **Short Circuit** 5.10 B
   35' QD's
   This one is *squeezed* between the previous two routes.

Bat Wall

1. **Hanging Tree** III 5.11 A (R) ★
   Multi-pitch   Pro to 3" including KB, LA, Rurps
   Notoriously loose and dirty in places, yet the upper portion of the climb offers excellent quality stemming and face climbing.

2. **Go Back to the Gym** I 5.7 A2 (First 30') ★★★
   30'   Pro to 1" includes TCU's, KB, LA Leepers, Hangers, Bathooks
   Super classic aid route of the *highest* standard. The second part called **Stay in the Gym** (II A3), branches onto a 1/4" deep tied-off pin stack seam ending with your arms around the tree. **Die in the Gym** (III A4+) goes up the overhung section on hooks (seven in a row), and b-a-a-ad pins to a sloping stance belay at 65'. Finish up the upper wall by criss-crossing the Hanging Tree route via free and aid to the summit anchor (160').

3. **Dracula** 5.12 A ★★★
   65'   10 QD's
   A premiere
   Broughton classic.
   Originally called the
   Unnamed Aid Route.
   Commence up a
   right-facing corner
   immediately right of
   the leaning tree.
   From a small ledge
   embark up a diagonal
   right leaning hand
   ramp, then up left,
   then right to a seam.
   Balance up the seam
   and surmount the
   final obstacle, a flared
   pea-pod corner. Bolt
   belay anchor.

4. **Bela Lugosi** 5.12 C
   ★★
   65'   10 QD's
   Fascinating route
   worthy of attention.
   Ascend a shallow
   corner gracefully to a
   thin stance. Pull
   through a desperately
   thin crux then up left
   via a zigzag seam

Mark Hudon at the roof on Bloodline (5.12B)

29

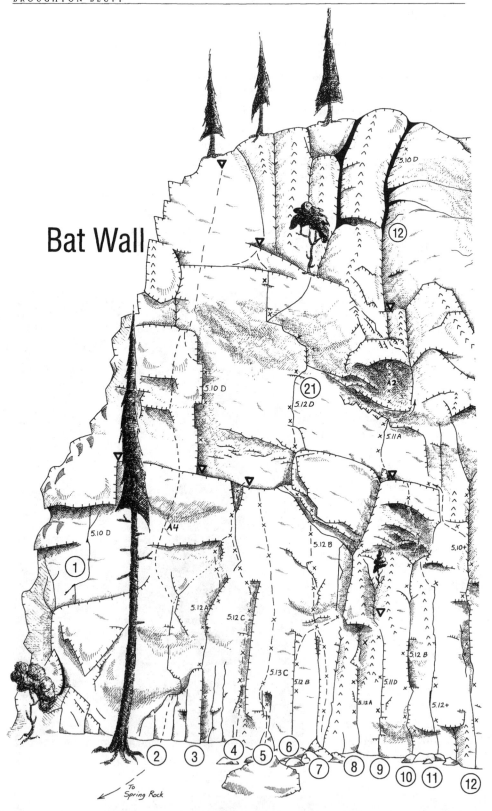

Bat Wall

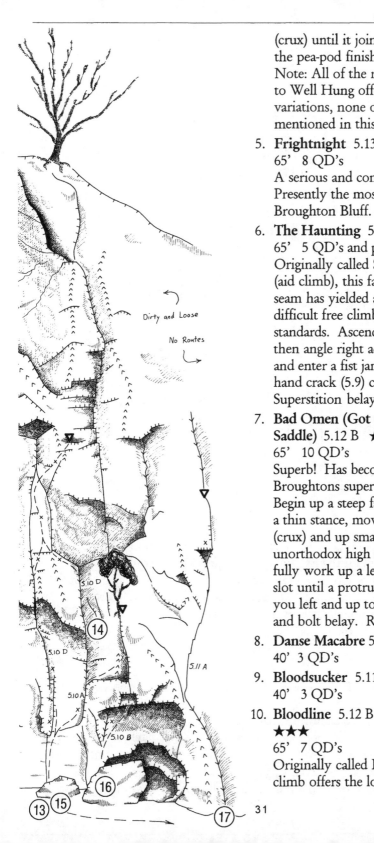

Dirty and Loose

No Routes

5.10 D

5.10 D

5.11 A

5.10 A

5.10 B

(14)

(13) (15)

(16)

(17)

(crux) until it joins with Dracula to the pea-pod finish.

Note: All of the routes from Dracula to Well Hung offer numerous variations, none of which are mentioned in this printing.

5. **Frightnight** 5.13 C
   65' 8 QD's
   A serious and committing climb. Presently the most difficult route at Broughton Bluff.

6. **The Haunting** 5.12 B ★
   65' 5 QD's and pro to 2"
   Originally called Snap, Crackle, Pop (aid climb), this fascinating vertical seam has yielded a sequential and difficult free climb of modern standards. Ascend the seam 25 ft., then angle right across Bad Omen and enter a fist jam that eases to a hand crack (5.9) corner ending at the Superstition belay anchor.

7. **Bad Omen (Got the Horse for My Saddle)** 5.12 B ★★★
   65' 10 QD's
   Superb! Has become one of Broughtons super classic face climbs. Begin up a steep face via sidepulls to a thin stance, move over the bulge (crux) and up small edges to an unorthodox high step (crux). Carefully work up a left leaning flared slot until a protruding roof forces you left and up to a sloping ledge and bolt belay. Rappel.

8. **Danse Macabre** 5.12
   40' 3 QD's

9. **Bloodsucker** 5.11 D
   40' 3 QD's

10. **Bloodline** 5.12 B
    ★★★
    65' 7 QD's
    Originally called Beeline, this gusto climb offers the local rockjock a bold

31

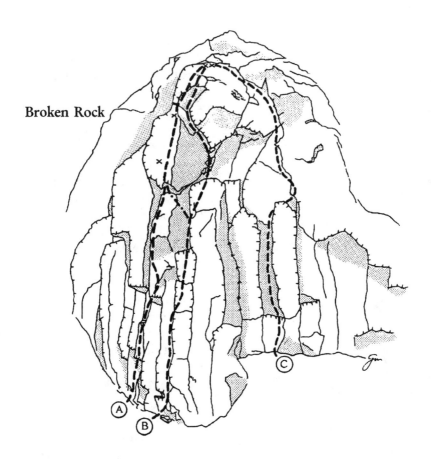

Broken Rock

Ⓐ Ⓑ Ⓒ

start and a fantastic roof to exit through. One of the most exciting and interesting routes on the Bat Wall. Layback up an overhung face to several natural pockets then crank up to a stance. Balance up a smooth section then up a thin crack to a stance below a large roof. Start on the right and power up left then over the lip and finally to the ledge and bolt belay for Superstition.

11. **Predator** 5.12 C
    60' QD's

12. **Superstition** III 5.11 A ★★★
    Multi-pitch   Pro to 2"
    First pitch QD's and minor pro to 1"
    A great route and quite popular, particularly the first pitch. Step up onto an outside corner and ascend a shallow groove corner system until possible to smear left via underclings (5.10+). Move up a thin crack then left along on a narrow ledge to a bolt anchor. Rappel or continue up the

vertical face above to the roof (the 1/4" bolt line out the roof is "Snap, Crackle, Pop") then fight (5.11 A) rightward around a corner and up to a belay ledge—or step right at the first belay and climb a second pitch direct start via 4 bolts (5.11 A). Continue up the corner above to a steep, nettle filled and surprisingly strenuous wide crack problem (5.10 D). Rappel with 2 ropes to the ground.

13. **Lost Boys** 5.10 D ★★
70' 8 QD's
A fun climb and an excellent warm-up. On the right side of the Bat Wall are several large boulders in front of a cave. Begin behind the left one, face climb up to an overhang (crux) with a slot. Move up, then right, mantle, then up until you can exit right via an undercling and reach (crux) around a corner to a bolt anchor on a ledge. Rappel.

14. **Mystic Pizza** (a.k.a. Mystic Direct) 5.10 D
70' QD's and pro to 1 1/2"
An interesting variation with good pro. Start as for Mystic Void; instead of traversing to the right to join Well Hung, continue up the obvious corner system then exit up left (crux) to join Lost Boys.

15. **Mystic Void** 5.10 A
45' Pro to 1"
Ascends the face left of, then joins with Well Hung just above the large roof. Rappel from bolts at the maple tree.

16. **Well Hung** 5.10 B ★★
45' Pro to 1"
An original Bat Wall favorite, even if it is a bit dirty. Step directly off the large boulders onto the face under the large roof. Traverse right then swing onto the roof via jug holds to a stance. Move up the corner to the bolt anchor at the maple tree. Rappel.

17. **Gold Arch** 5.11 A
70' Pro to 3"
At one time a fantastic line, but getting dirtier every year due to soil erosion from the field above the cliff. Start 30' right of Well Hung and ascend a slab then a strenuous barn door lieback on a gold-streaked wall. Belay. The second pitch leads to easier ground above.

18. **The Hunger** 5.11 D
55' Pro to 1 1/2" Cams suggested
Physically difficult route, but a little dirty.

19. **Dark Shadows** 5.10 D ★
40' Pro to 1 1/2" TCU's recommended
Originally called Shadow Dancing (5.8 A2), this climb was easily freed to produce a unique problem. Ascend a face to a left facing corner capped by a large roof. Step left, then up, then left (crux) past fixed pitons and up to a belay anchor on a small ledge. Rappel.

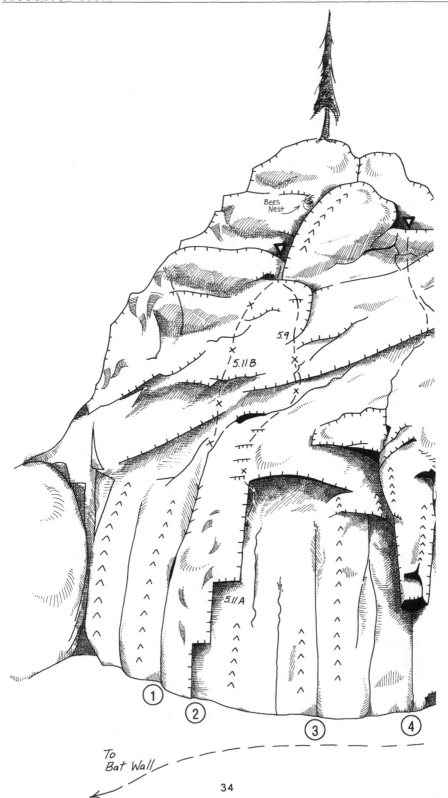

Bees
Nest

5.9

5.11 B

5.11 A

① ② ③ ④

To
Bat Wall

34

Trinity Wall

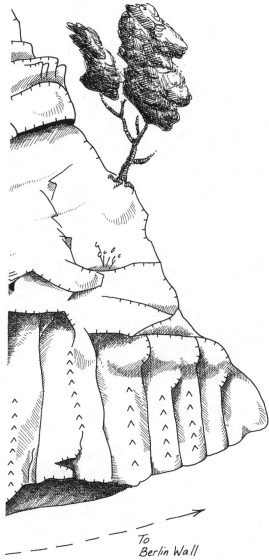

To
Berlin Wall

The following routes are located on the upper headwall of the Bat Wall.

20.

21. **Manson Family Reunion**
5.12 D ★★
60' 7 QD's

22. **Vampyr** 5.11 C / D
Pro QD's
This bolt route climbs up left from first pitch belay on Superstition.

23. **Remain in Light** 5.11 D
Pro QD's
Where Superstition moves left on the first pitch crux, this route instead continues up the corner, then steps right onto Lost Boys, then continues up and left to merge with the same route at the next belay.

24.

25.

Immediately south of the Bat Wall are several outcrops of rock. First is a blocky short vertical chunk known as Broken Rock. Follow the trail beyond this outcrop to other selections of rock at the 'end of the world' Welcome to the hidden walls of Broughton Bluff, steeped in mystery and tall tale.

Broken Rock

A. **Static Cling** 5.11 A
35' pro to 3/4", small TCU's
Height a factor when moving past the first bolt. Variation using Plan B route is 5.10 D.

B. **Plan B** 5.10 A
35' pro to 2", 1 1/2" Friend

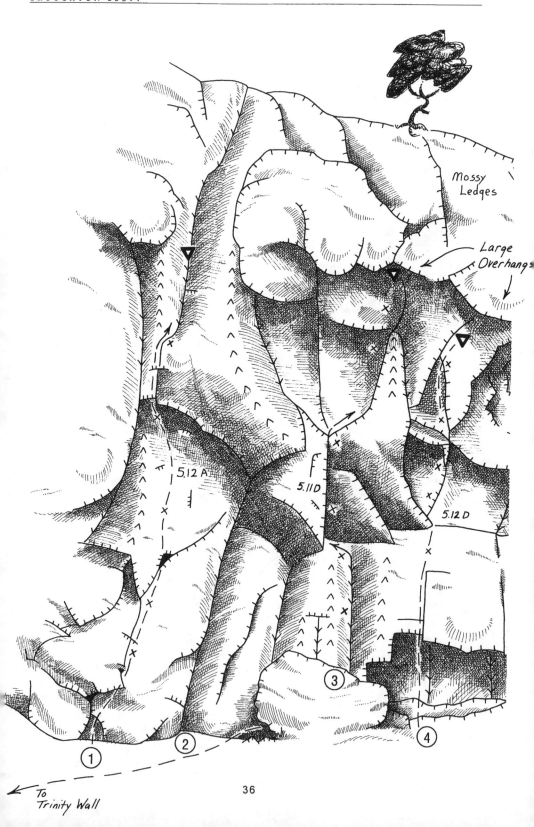

Mossy Ledges

Large Overhang

5.12 A

5.11 D

5.12 D

① ② ③ ④

To Trinity Wall

Berlin Wall

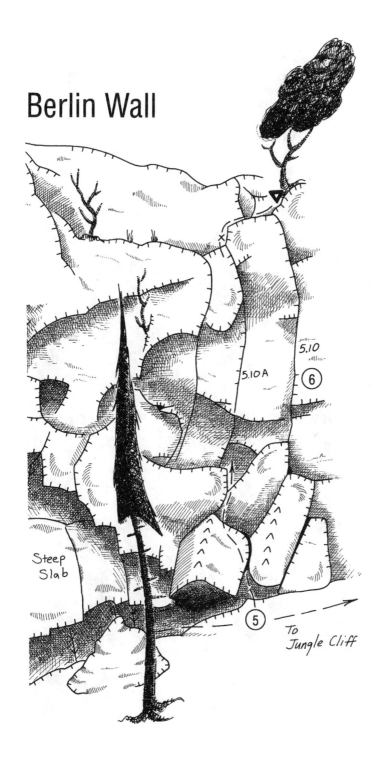

5.10

5.10A

6

Steep
Slab

5

To
Jungle Cliff

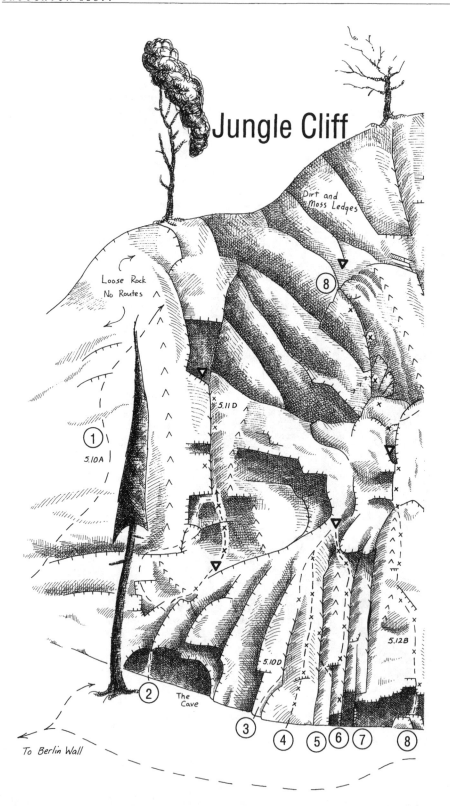

Jungle Cliff

Dirt and Moss Ledges

Loose Rock
No Routes

⑧

5.11 D

① 5.10A

② The Cave

⑧

5.12B

5.10D

③ ④ ⑤ ⑥ ⑦ ⑧

To Berlin Wall

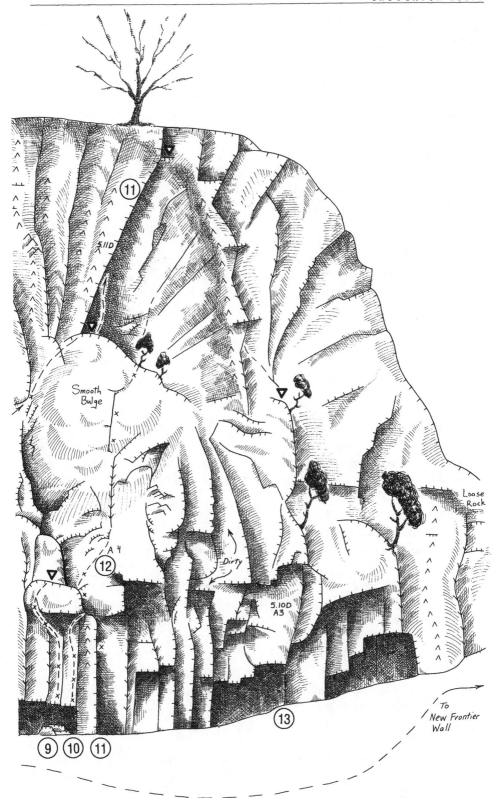

⑪

5.11D

Smooth
Bulge

Loose
Rock

A 4
⑫

Dirty

5.10D
A3

⑬

To
New Frontier
Wall

⑨ ⑩ ⑪

and a 0 TCU recommended

C. **Lickety Split** 5.6 ★
35' pro to 2", including a 3 1/2" Friend
Fun route.

Trinity Wall

1. **Bust A Move** 5.11 B ★
40' 4 QD's and pro to 1"
Terrific climb with a surprising crux. Commence up a shallow corner then over a minor bulge. Angle rightward via thin holds and underclings (crux), then up an easy corner to a bolt anchor. Rappel.

2. **Father** 5.11 A ★
40' Pro to 1 1/2"
Quality climb. Ascend the strenuous right-facing corner until possible to exit up left onto a slab. Move up right on easy ground then up left (bolt) in the center of the face, and left to the bolt anchor in a corner. Rappel.

3. _____
40' (TR)

4. _____
40' (TR)

Berlin Wall

1. **Closet Nazi** 5.12 A ★★
45' 5 QD's
Remarkable and highly challenging route. Climb the bolt line on the left side of the wall up very clean, overhung rock. Can be a virtual stream of water during the winter months.

2. **Recipe for Airtime** II A3
30' Pitons and natural pro

3. **Twist and Crawl** 5.11 D
40' 5 QD's
Located in the center of the wall directly under the huge roof. Unusual yet quite good. Move up a dihedral around a crux corner then up and out the overhang to the anchor. Rappel.

4. **Genocide** 5.12 D /.13 A
40' 5 QD's
To the right of Twist and Crawl is another route on this virtually upside down wall. Start up a crack on a slab then up via physically articulate moves out the overhang to a bolt anchor.

5. **Pride and Joy** 5.10 A
40' Pro to 1" Small wires recommended
On the far right side of Berlin Wall is a smooth vertical section of rock

broken with several thin cracks. The left is a 5.10 A, the right is a top-rope. Takes good pro. Rappel from the tree anchor directly above the top-rope problem.

6. _____ 5.10

  40' (TR)

Jungle Cliff

The next two crags are located on private land. The Jungle Cliff has a layer of thinly caked dirt due to water runoff from the farmers field above the wall, especially from the center of the wall to the right side.

1. **Zimbabwe** II 5.10 A
   Multi-pitch Pro to 3" Cams recommended
   Ascends the steep face on the far left corner of Jungle Cliff via numerous ledges.

2. **Slash and Burn** 5.12 A
   60' QD's and minor pro to 2"
   A good route on fantastic steep rock. Begin at the cave, pull up (5.9), move up the slab to the right, then up the face to an anchor. Continue up the overhanging corner above, move left at difficult section and finish up a vertical dihedral to a final crux move. Rappel from bolt anchor.

3. **Under the Yum Yum Tree** 5.10 D
   50' Pro to 2" Needs bolts
   Fun climb with an appropriate name. Start to the right of the cave and ascend a dusty slab via a thin crack and corner system to a bolt anchor.

4. **Tarzan** 5.12 D
   50' 7 QD's
   The obvious and impressive arete. Tarzan is definitely one of the most unusual routes of this kind at Broughton Bluff. Worth the blast.

5. **Crime Wave** 5.10 C
   50' QD's, TCU's, #2 Friend recommended
   A slightly awkward variation next to Gorilla Love Affair.

6. **Gorilla Love Affair**
   5.10 D ★★★
   50' 6 QD's, optional TCU's
   A very popular climb. Well protected yet exhilarating. Stem up to a small roof, move left, then up to another roof. Step right and up a smooth dihedral (crux) until possible to step left to finish up a crack leading to the bolt belay for Under the Yum Yum Tree. Rappel.

7. **Out of Africa** II 5.9 A3

8. **Heart of Darkness** 5.12 B ★★
   80' 10 QD's
   A beautiful route that leads up an overhung arete in the heart of Jungle Cliff country. Desperately struggle out the overhung start to a stance,

New Frontier Cliff

5.11 A

Smooth
Face

5.10 D

Dirt
Gully

Moss
Covered
Ledges

① ②

To
Jungle Cliff

5.10 C

5.11 C

4

Gully

5.10 A

5.11 B

3

5

6

7

Poison Oak

then up and left along a hand ramp. Pull through the crux (thin) then up the right side of the arete to a stance. Make a quick move up a smooth face and up to a tiny stance belay. Proceed up left out the fiercely overhung headwall (5 bolts and 5.11 D) via face and jug holds. Rappel with 2 ropes.

⊗. **Mowgli Direct** 5.12 B
40' QD's
Located between Heart of Darkness and Mowgli's Revenge.

9. **Mowgli's Revenge** 5.11 B
40' 4 QD's
Underneath a large roof to the right of Heart of Darkness, you will find two bolt routes. The left one is Mowgli's Revenge. An interesting climb that exits the roof on the left side. Rappel from bolt anchor.

10. **Amazon Woman** 5.10 D ★
40' 4 QD's and minor pro to 1 1/2" Cams recommended
Commence up a vertical stem problem via small edges to a stance. Reach up right under the roof, then traverse right and exit to a good stance. Step up a wide crack to a huge ledge and bolt belay. Rappel.

11. **Amazon Man** III 5.11 A3 (or 5.11D) ★★★
Multi-pitch Pro to 3" Need KB, LA
This staggering and original achievement, put up in 1979, penetrates through the heart of Jungle Cliff. Begin up a corner (immediately right of Amazon Woman) past a fixed piton to a stance, then up a wide crack to a big ledge with a good anchor. Mowgli's Revenge joins here. Continue up by one of two cracks to a stance, then delicately traverse left via sloping ledges (bolts) to the Heart of Darkness belay. Ascend directly above you (5.10+) to another belay then move right around the sweet headwall and up a difficult section. Belay at bolts on Skull Ledge. Storm the dihedral (5.11 D) directly above that leads to the summit. Monkey Paws route (5.11 B) is the face climb at right side of skull ledge. Rappel with 2 ropes.

12. **Killer Pygmy** III 5.10+ A4 ★
Multi-pitch Pro to 4" Cams, TCU's, KB, LA, Angles and bolts
Outrageous aid line that boldly pushes up the smooth center face to Skull Ledge. The final pitch angles up right via two optional cracks (A2).

13. **Mujahideen** II 5.10 D A3
80' Pro to 4" including KB, LA, and Angles

New Frontier Cliff

1. **Luck of the Draw** 5.11 A
80' QD's and pro to 1"

⊗. **Touch and Go** (variation start for both routes) 5.10 C
80' QD's and pro to 1"

2. **Alma Mater** 5.10 D ★★★
80' QD's

Beautiful steep slab on the left side of New Frontier Cliff. Commence up an odd balance start (5.10 D) until it eases to a continuous, fun 5.8 climb ending on a ledge. Rappel.

⊗. **Split Decision** 5.8
30' Pro to 4"
Climb the wide crack immediately right of Alma Mater.

⊗. **Tin Star** 5.8
60' Pro = small wires
Climb the outside of the block to the belay ledge, then continue up left onto a face (bolts) and up to an anchor.

⊗. **True Grit** 5.9
80' Pro to 2"
From the top of the block step up left into dihedral and up this to top.

⊗. **Pony Express** 5.6
30' Pro to 2"
This is the route on the right side of the block.

Dave Sowerby climbing Heart of Darkness (5.12B)

45

3. **Happy Trails** II 5.10 A
   Multi-pitch   Pro to 3"
   Interesting climb with some grungy, loose sections. Walk to the right side
   of the wall (trail's end). Above is a short clean jam crack that pulls
   through a slot to a left-facing slab corner. Climb this and enter into a loose
   chimney then belay at the oak tree. Continue up right a few moves until
   you can undercling left then up a broken slab above to top out. Rappel or
   walk off.

4. **Wild Wild West** 5.10 C
   60'   Pro to 3" Cams suggested
   Climb the first pitch of Happy Trails. From the oak tree, step left to a
   crack then up to a large roof. Undercling out right (crux) and around
   corner (rope jams easily) then up easy cracks to the top.

5. **Pioneer Spirit** 5.11 B ★
   45'   4 QD's and minor pro to 1"
   Climb the short, clean jam crack of Happy Trails. Step right and then up
   this tantalizing face climb. The crux is a blind lunge. Rappel from bolt
   anchor.

6. **Promised Land** 5.11 C (R) ★
   80'   Pro to 3" Cams and small wires (RP's) recommended
   Superb climb on beautiful rock, yet located virtually "at the end of the
   world." Start to the right of Happy Trails and behind several trees. Pull
   up an easy bulge, move up left on a slab to a vertical step. From a ledge,
   climb the exciting and steep crack system to a huge block. Lean out right
   (bolt) and layback up the arete to a bolt anchor. Route is totally over-
   grown.

Rocky Butte Quarry

This urban rock butte offers easy access and a central location in NE Portland. Located adjacent to I-205, the Butte in recent years has become a very popular afternoon climbing area. Many people visit the crag each year to learn technique and to top-rope the more than 100 climbs.

Extensive and secluded, this north facing crag is comfortably hidden amongst a tall, green canopied forest. Used infrequently during the 1950's and 1960's, it was the 1970's that heralded a new era. Several established climbs received recognition, such as **Blackberry Jam** (5.10 A) in 1974 by Jim Davis and T. Crossman, located on the White Rabbit Buttress. **Expresso** (5.9) and, **White Rabbit** (5.10) in 1977, **Birds of Paradise** (5.10 C) in 1979, **Toothpick** (5.11 C), **Close to the Edge** (5.11+), and **Blueberry Jam** (5.10 A) were soon to follow. Those young people who proved instrumental during the 70's phase were key to the future of climbing here. Doug Bower, Bill Coe, Jay Kerr, Robert McGown, Mike Smelsar, John Sprecher, Scott Woolums and others developed rock climbing as a traditional sport at the Butte. Though the crag fell quiet from 1979 to 1984, these same persons and others such as Mike Pajunas, Wayne Wallace, Joe Parsley, Gary Rall and others eventually tamed the Rocky Butte 'frontier' in the late 1980's.

Scores of urban classics were produced. **Bite the Bullet** (5.11 A), **Fandango** (5.10 C), **Live Wire** (5.11 A), **Edge of Might** (5.11 B), **Stranger than Friction** (5.10 A) **Ziva's** (5.10 B), **Phylynx** (5.11 B), **Wizard** (5.11 A), **Crack Warrior** (5.11 B), **Emotional Rescue** (5.10 B), **Vertical Therapy** (5.9), **Red Zinger** (5.11 C) and many more.

The Quarry is generally a top-rope area. Virtually all of the routes have been led at one time, but now, since much of the original fixed gear has been removed, top-roping is the name of the game. Those few routes that are still leadable are well worth it, such as **Emotional Rescue**, **Phylynx**, or **Wizard**. Do bring extra slings to use as extensions from the nearest tree anchor.

The Quarry environment does have several drawbacks. Poison oak, spray paint, litter and noise from the I-205 freeway are the most obvious. Yet this crag is very accessible to the public, especially for the local rock jock escaping the office blues.

Thanks to the tiny sparks cast from the **Rocky Butte Quarry Guide** (1987) by Robert McGown and Mike Pajunas, climber interest at this crag has increased rapidly. Trails have improved with use, the climbs are cleaner and the general image of Rocky Butte has changed for the better.

There are 16 sections of wall at the Butte. The following are described left to right as if facing the crag: Poodle Pinnacle, Trivial Pinnacle, Silver Bullet Bluff, Video Bluff, New Era Cliff, Dream Weaver Wall, Wizard Wall, Far East Wall, Warrior Wall, Freeway Wall, Mean Street, Easy Street, Toothpick Wall, Breakfast Cracks, Wall of Shadows and the Grotto area.

Silver Bullet Bluff

To reach the cliffs, take the 82nd Ave. exit (eastbound) from I-84 and drive north to the intersection of Freemont and 82nd. Turn right (east), drive approximately 1/2 mile. The roadcurves north to become 91st street, (eventually to loop clockwise around to the top of Rocky Butte). The cliffs are located on the north side of the road near the Bible Temple Church "domes." There are several obvious dirt pullouts available. The top of Rocky Butte offers several fun boulder traverse problems to strenghten the fingertips. The views from the top of the butte are exceptional, both of the City of Roses and the surrounding mountains.

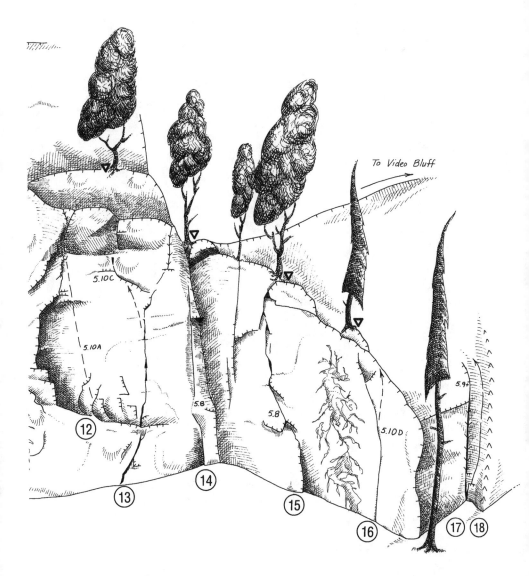

Poodle Pinnacle

1. **Poodle with a Mohawk** 5.11 A
   Pro to 2 1/2"
   A neat climb located by itself along the eastern perimeter trail. Hike
   approximately 300 ft. along the trail. Above the trail is a face with an easy
   start, a crack and an outside arete. Lead this to a tree. Rappel.

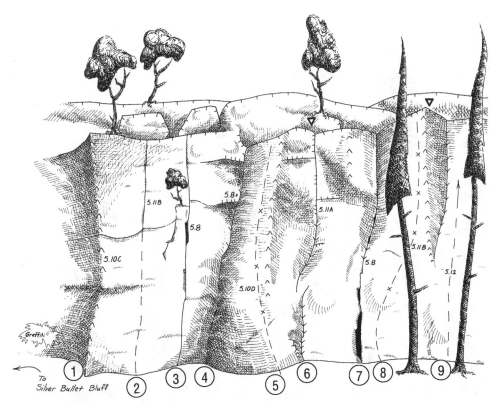

Trivial Pinnacle

Hike east on a perimeter trail to the tunnel under the road. Angle north toward the cliff.

1. **Harlequin** 5.10 B ★
   Pro to 1 1/2"
   A good climb. Commence up an easy start then angle right up the curved crack (25 ft.) until it eases near the top. Belay at tree.

2. **Trivial Pursuit** 5.10 B
   Pro to 1 1/2"
   A minor face climb just to the right.

3. **The Joker** 5.8

Silver Bullet Bluff

Named because of all the bullet scars dotting the face of this elusive crag. Approach by hiking east along the perimeter trail to the tunnel under the roadway. Aim north to the crag and down, step 20 ft. to a large ledge. Belay here for the routes in the main wall below. Height approximately 35 to 40 ft.

1. _____ 5.10+ (TR)

Video Bluff

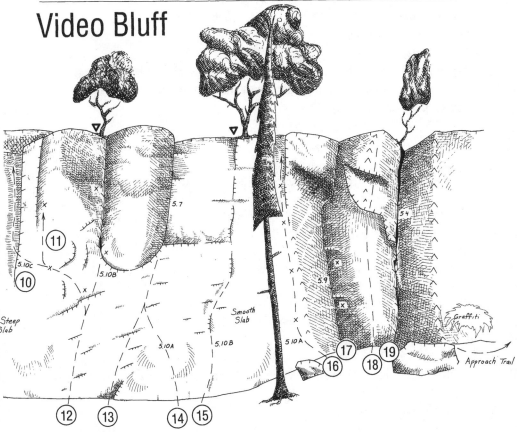

2. **Captain She's Breaking Up** 5.8 (R)
   Pro to 2"

3. _____

4. **Sundance Kid** 5.10 A
   Neat shallow corner climb on upper left corner of Silver Bullet Bluff.

5. **Panama Red** 5.9+
   Climb the smooth face broken with small edges and cracks immediately right of Sundance Kid.

6. **Miss Kitty** 5.7

7. **Gunsmoke** 5.9 ★★
   An excellent easy face climb just left of Bite the Bullet.

8. **Bite the Bullet** 5.11 A (R) ★★★
   One of the best routes on Silver Bullet Bluff. Start up left of a tree and on a face with good but angled edges. From a good stance 15 ft. up angle left onto a bullet-scarred face and climb desperately to a sloping ledge, then more up right to join with the last move on Jack of Hearts.

9. **Jack of Heart** 5.9+ ★★★
   Pro to 1"
   An exciting thin crack climb. Start up a short right facing corner to a

stance. Then up a thin crack to a sloping ledge. Finish up a last vertical step to the belay ledge.

10. **Silver Bullet** 5.9 (R)
A good route that starts up the face, then enters a dihedral that is lacking a crack. Smear up the corner to join with Jack of Hearts.

11. **Urban Cowboy** 5.8 (R)

12. **Last Tango** 5.10 A

13. **Fandango** 5.10 C (R) ★★★
A superb route of only moderate difficulty. Start up a crack on a slab left of a main corner. From an easy stance continue up the crack on the vertical face, follow the left crack and pull a mantle (crux). Move up further via a corner to a ledge. Belay from the large tree above.

14. **Midnight Warrior** 5.8
Pro to 2"
The main corner on this side of the wall.

15. **Superman Crack** 5.8 (R) ★
Pro to 1"
A fun problem on good edges and sloping smears.

16. **Centurion** 5.10 D ★
A unique short vertical crack problem on the lower right corner of this wall. Climb the crack until you can reach over right (crux) and up to easy steps and tree belay.

17. **Invisible Man** 5.9+

18. **Temporary Arete** 5.10 A

Video Bluff

One of the two most popular walls frequented at Rocky Butte. Excellent place to top-rope and learn technique. Approach Video Bluff by parking at the easternmost pullout (just before the **stone** guardrail) and aim north to the crag. A well beaten trail starts here and loops along the crag west to emerge at the guardrail descent trail. Height approximately 35 ft.

1. **Body Language** 5.10 C (R)
The overhanging arete with a horizontal crack halfway up.

2. **Body Bionics** 5.11 B (R)

3. **Ace** 5.8

4. **Eve of Destruction** 5.8+
A slabby dihedral problem. A good practice climb.

5. **Live Wire** 5.10 D ★★
4 QD's
Excellent difficult face problem on the round outside corner right of Eve of Destruction. A must for everyone.

6. **Damaged Circuit** 5.11 A ★★
Challenging stem problem up a shallow scoop. Begin up a shattered start, pull a thin move to an awkward stance, then smear, stem up a face using strange finger holds in the seam.

7. **Robotics** 5.8

8. **Edge of Might** 5.11 B ★★
Fantastic climb. Begin up the face immediately right of Robotics and angle up onto the arete. Thin holds and pinches on the arete are the crux.

9. **Hard Contact** 5.12 C

10. **Lever or Leaver** 5.10 C

11. **Persistence of Time** 5.11 C
3 QD's

12. **Zeeva** 5.10 B ★★
3 QD's
A popular climb with a narrow dihedral crux section. Climb up the slabby face on good holds to a large hold below the corner. Reach and stem up the corner to the top. Fun route.

13. **Flakey Old Man** 5.7 ★★
The flake has long since fallen away but the popularity of this and the routes nearby make it a favorite.

14. **MTV** 5.10 A
Boulder problem variation.

15. **Stranger Than Friction** 5.10 B ★★★
In the center of the slab is a pocketed boulder start and slap move leading upward to a seam. The local classic favorite on this wall and certainly worth it.

16. **Panes of Reality** 5.10 A ★
4 QD's
Step left and up onto the face immediately left of Stained Glass. A neat problem on a rounded bulge.

17. **Stained Glass** 5.9 ★
QD's and pro to 2"
Obvious fun dihedral corner.

18. **Toxic Waltz** 5.11D
4 QD's
Vertical face to the right of the dihedral.

19. **E-Z Corner** 5.4

Dream Weaver Wall

This is a narrow section of wall located between Video Bluff and Wizard Wall. These climbs are good though infrequently ascended. Height is approximately 65 ft.

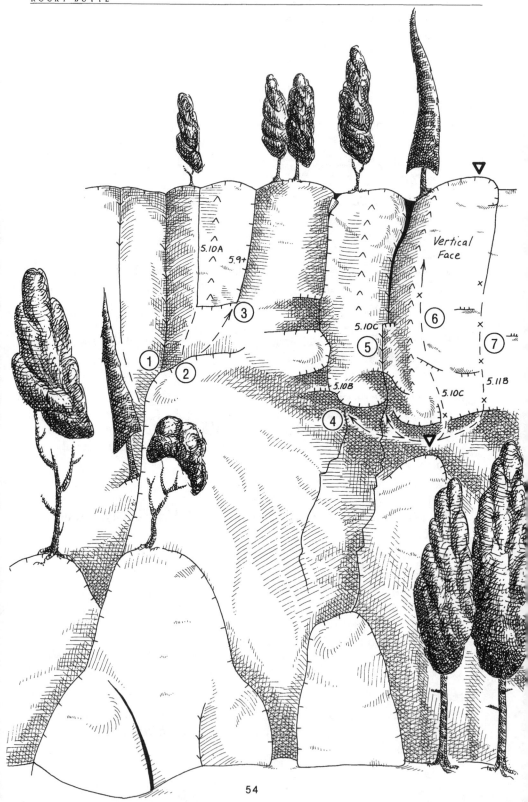

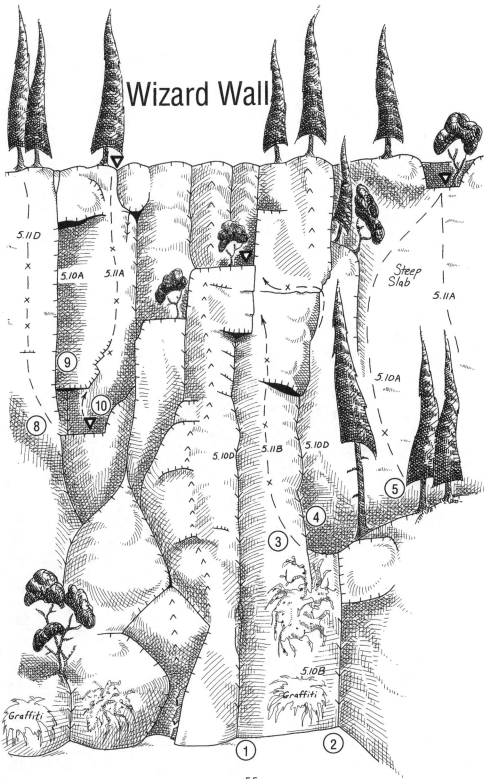

Wizard Wall

5.11D

5.10A   5.11A

9

8   10

5.10D   5.11B   5.10D

3

4

5.10B

Graffiti

Graffiti

1   2

Steep Slab

5.11A

5.10A

5

55

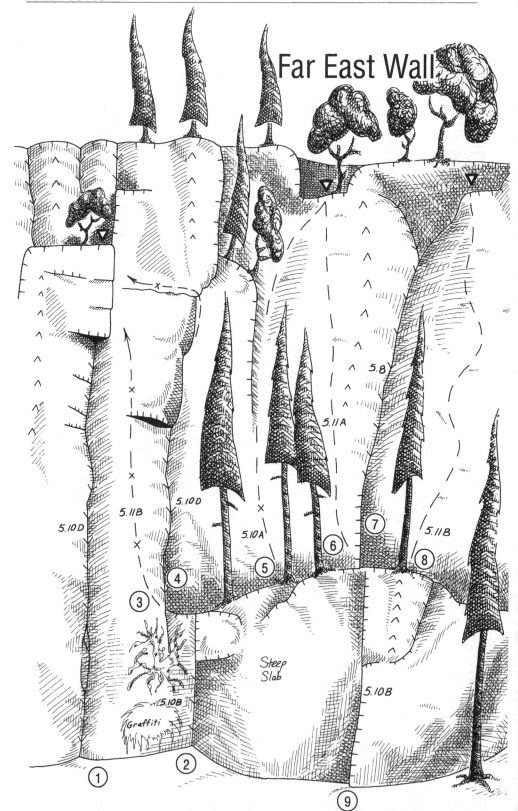

Far East Wall

5.8

5.11A

5.10D

5.11B

5.10D

5.10A

5.11B

⑦

⑥

⑧

⑤

④

③

Steep
Slab

5.10B

5.10B

Graffiti

①

②

⑨

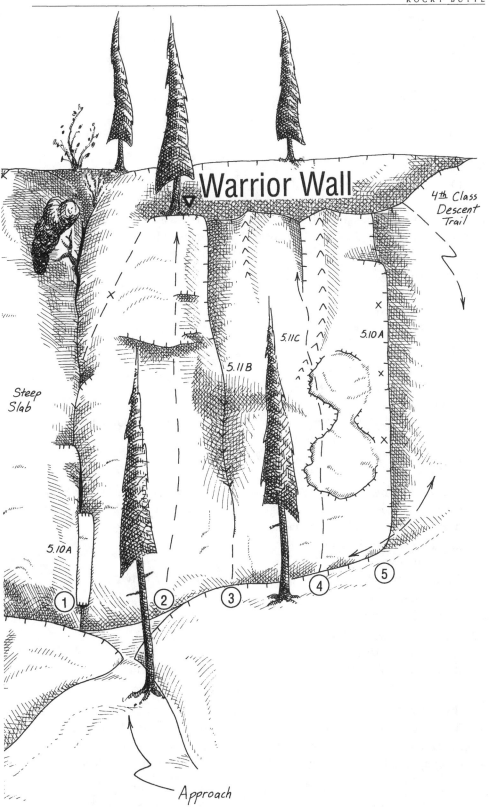

Warrior Wall

4th Class Descent Trail

5.10 A

5.11 C

5.11 B

Steep Slab

5.10 A

① ② ③ ④ ⑤

Approach

1. **Dream Weaver** 5.9 ★
Pro to 2"
2. **Head Bangers Ball** 5.10 A
Pro to 1 1/2"
3. **Tiger's Pause** 5.9 ★
Pro to 2"
4. **Kleen Korner** 5.9

Wizard Wall

One of the finest long vertical sections of rock at the Butte. All of the routes are located on the upper half of the wall. Either top-rope from trees at the top of the cliff or rappel down approximately 60 to 80 ft. to bolt anchors or ledges and then lead back up. This wall is of superb quality, yielding some of the finest high angle face climbs at Rocky Butte.

1. **Kleen Korner** 5.9
2. **Naked Savage** 5.10 A
3. **Lord of the Jungle** 5.9+ (variation)
4. **Slavemaker** 5.10 B
5. **Grub** 5.10 C
Pro to 3" Cams suggested
6. **Eye in the Sky** 5.10 C (R) ★
Pro to 1"
Start at the Phylynx belay, but stay just to the left of the route on an outside corner after the bulge crux.
7. **Phylynx** 5.11 B ★★★
Pro to 1 1/2"
One of the finest routes at Rocky Butte. Rappel to a hidden anchor 80 ft. down on the left, then lead up right (bolts), pull through bulge (crux) then directly up the crack on the face.
8. **Walk on Water** 5.11 D ★
QD's and pro to 1"
An impressive and extreme face route to the right of Phylynx.
9. **Mind Games** 5.10 A
Offwidth Chimney.
10. **Wizard** 5.11 A ★★★
QD's and pro to 1"
Excellent climb on a beautiful rock. Dynamic and unusual.

Far East Wall

This hidden corner of wall is the westerly extension of the Wizard Wall. Approach by rappeling in from the tree at the top of Seventh Moon or scramble up a 3rd class trail from the bottom. Forty ft. to halfway terrace,

100 ft. approximate total height.

1. **The Wanderer** 5.10 D ★
2. **Great Wall of China** 5.10 B ★
3. **High Road to China** 5.11 B
4. **Chinese Finger Torture** 5.10 D ★
5. **Ghost Rider** 5.10 A
6. **Flight of the Seventh Moon** 5.11 A ★★
   A neat, challenging face climb that goes up just left of the Orient Express dihedral and ends at the tree belay.
7. **Orient Express** 5.8 ★
   Dihedral located at the center of the face.
8. **Secret Maze** 5.11 B ★
   A difficult face climb. Start to the right of the dihedral and climb up (crux) to a stance, then meander up the face using holds that seem to be in all the wrong places. Captain Granite said so.
9. **Tigers Eye** 5.10 B
   Fun direct start leading to the terraced ledges below Orient Express.

Warrior Wall

An extension of the Far East Wall, it was coined because of the favorite difficult corner problem here. Casually referred to as the "Bug Wall." One can descend via the standard guardrail descent trail next to the chainlink fence. Approximate height ranges from 45 to 100 ft.

1. **Smears for Fears** 5.10 A
   Pro to 2"
   A good crack climb further right of Secret Maze. Ends at the large fir tree on a ledge.
2. _____ 5.13 TR
   The extreme face climb just left of Crack Warrior.
3. **Crack Warrior** 5.11 B (R) ★★★
   Pro to 1 1/2"
   A great climb with a nasty crux. Silverfish frequent here. Climb the corner stem problem up to a bulge (crux). Pull through and move up an easier right facing corner to the large fir tree. Belay.
4. **You'll Dance to Anything** 5.11 C (TR) ★★
   Beautiful face climb that makes use of a broken section of smooth rock. The exit is the crux due to numerous sloping finger edges.
5. **Sheer Madness** 5.10 A 3 QD's
6. **Quarry Cracker** 5.6
7. **Lathe of Heaven** 5.11 A
8. **Arch Nemesis** 5.11 A ★
   Pro to 1 1/2" including pitons

A major dihedral on this face. Climb up the vertical corner until possible to step out right and up a flake that leads to a large fir tree.

9. **Boy Sage** 5.10+ (variation)
   Pro to 1 1/2" including pitons
   Take the direct up a crack to the tree.

10. **Jealous Rage** 5.11 C (R)
    Pro to 1"
    Leads up an indistinct face (bolts) left to join with Arch Nemesis.

11. **Emotional Rescue** 5.10 B ★★★
    QD's and pro to 2"
    One of the finest classics at the Butte. Very popular. Climb the steep bolt and pin protected face to exit up a crack and a bolt anchor hidden around corner. Rappel.

Freeway Wall

Approximate height ranges from 20 to 40 ft.

1. **Simple Twist** 5.11
2. **Hyper Twist** 5.11
3. **Passing Lane** 5.6
4. **Speeding Down South** 5.8
5. **Ranger Danger** 5.9+
6. **Telegraph Road** 5.11 A (TR)
7. **Highway Star** 5.10 C ★
   Pro to 1 1/2"
   A good crack climb with a strenuous exit move.
8. **Dead Man's Curve** 5.9

Mean Street

This steep wall is situated directly below the guardrail adjacent to the road. The routes are characterized by difficult, hard to protect and usually dust-covered rock. Height approximately 100 ft.

1. **Thunder Road** 5.10 A
2. **Lethal Ethics** 5.10 D (R)
   Poorly protected face climb intersected by a ledge halfway up.
3. **Spiritual Journey** 5.10 D
   Ascend the face just left of a minor arete and continue up an inside corner leading to the top.
4. **Little Arete** 5.9 (R)
5. **Seamingly Endless** 5.11 B ★
   Pro to 1"
   Start on the right side of the arete and zig zag up discontinuous cracks and corners to the top.

Warrior Wall - Lower Right

Guardrail
Descent
Trail

9 5.11A

5.10+

5.10B

5.11C

5.11A

Graffiti

8

10

7

11

To
Freeway Wall

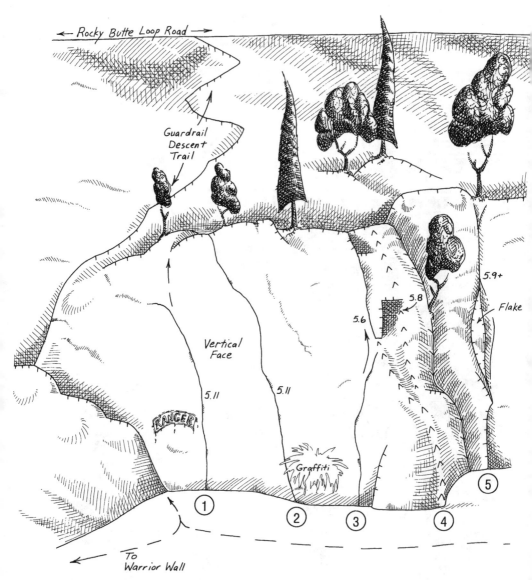

6. **Holy Bubbles** 5.11 B ★
   Start to the right of the arete, ascend up and over a roof, then up an inside corner to a belay anchor. Rappel.

7. **Pluto** 5.12 B
   A bolted face left of the "nose". A bit runout, strenuous, a little dusty. Has yet to see a free ascent.

8. **Stump the Jock** 5.11+
   The crack and inside corner just left of the prominent "nose" of rock. Begin up and angle left up an overhang corner until possible to turn the crux and continue up a steep wall above. Pull another small roof and

Freeway Wall

rappel from trees just above. Dirty.

9. **Packin' Heat** 5.13 A
QD's
The prominent "nose" of rock.

10. **No Leverage** 5.11 C
Could be a good climb, but the new drainage ditch pours down immediately to the right. Begin up a bolt and pin protected face to a corner and traverse directly left just below a large detached flake of rock to a bolt belay. Rappel.

11. **Be Bold or Not to Be** 5.11 C
A true blue water course now.

Mean Street

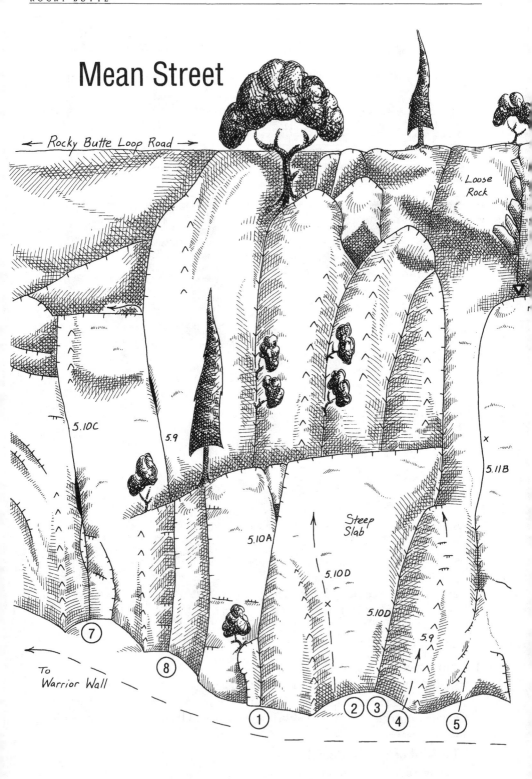

← Rocky Butte Loop Road →

Loose Rock

5.10C

5.9

5.11B

Steep Slab

5.10A

5.10D

5.10D

5.9

⑦

To Warrior Wall

⑧

① ② ③ ④ ⑤

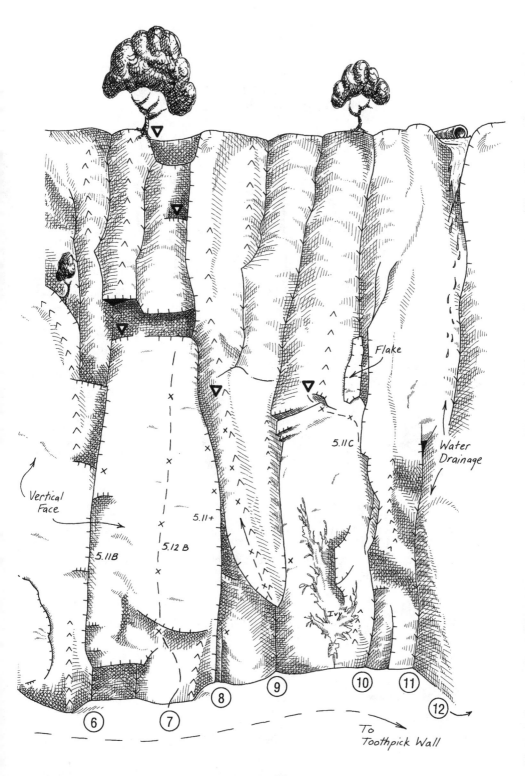

Vertical
Face

5.11B

5.12 B

5.11+

Flake

5.11C

Water
Drainage

Ivy

⑥ ⑦ ⑧ ⑨ ⑩ ⑪ ⑫

To
Toothpick Wall

Toothpick Wall

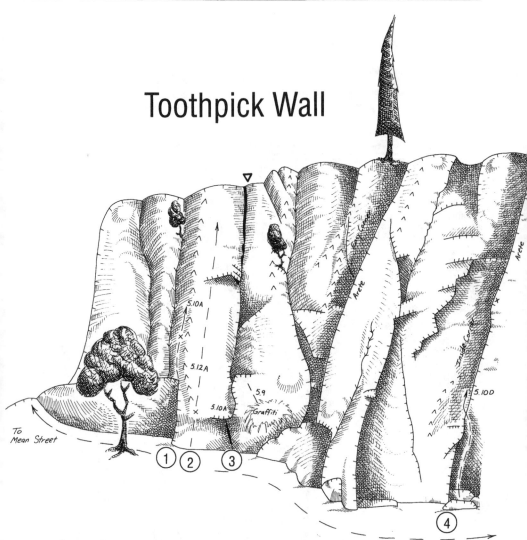

12. **Claymation** 5.10 C
    A crack corner system to the right of the water course. May be dusty, but
    still feasible to climb.

Easy Street

A good practice wall to teach rappelling and top-roping to novices. Approximately 35 ft. high.

A. **Hand Crack** 5.7

B. **Face** 5th Class

C. **Chimney** 5th Class

D. **Face / Finger** 5.9

E. **Chimney** 5.2 Descent trail approach for this area.

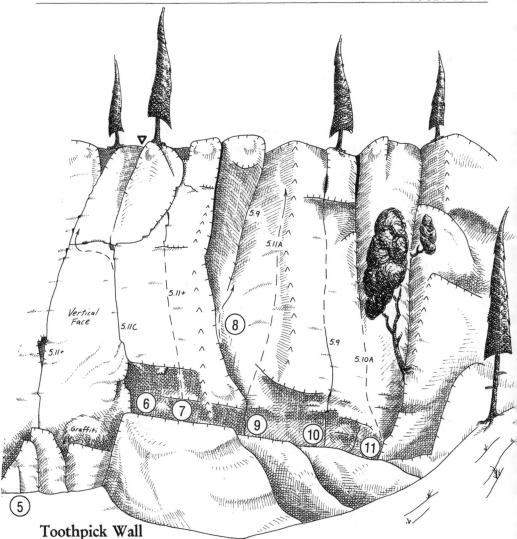

Toothpick Wall

A beautiful, colorful wall. Characterized by clean, steep rock and several incredible thin crack routes. Approximate height 50 ft.

1. **Reach for the Sky** 5.10 A ★

   Pro to 2"

   A fun climb. Ascend via a crack start then an outside corner until possible to move to the right side of the arete and top out. (1 pin - 1 bolt)

2. **Zenith** 5.12 A (TR)

3. **Blueberry Jam** 5.9 (5.10 A boulder start) ★★★

   Pro to 3"

   A very popular practice climb. Start to the right or do the direct boulder start, then ascend to the top via a broken crack system and large holds.

⊗. **Joy Ride** 5.11 A

   Bolted face climb to the right of Blueberry Jam.

4. **Leading Edge** 5.10 D
A corner to face arete system to the left of Close to the Edge.

5. **Close to the Edge** 5.11+ ★★★
Excellent climb on superb rock involving strenuous technique. Climb a thin crack that diagonals up rightward.

6. **Toothpick** 5.11 C ★★★
The local classic, one of Rocky Butte's finest. Start on a ledge, step up left onto the vertical face via awkward holds. Either traverse left on a horizontal crack to finish up via Close to the Edge (the standard method) or climb straight up a crack-seam to the top (harder).

7. **Far from the Edge** 5.11+ (TR) ★

8. **Rob's Ravine** 5.9
Pro to 3"
A deep dihedral to the right of Toothpick.

9. **Competitive Edge** 5.11 A
Kind of interesting, not quite so easy to follow the arete.

10. **Vertical Therapy** 5.9 ★★
Pro to 3"
Ascend via a crack leading to a face, then finish up a crack near the top. An excellent climb and a must for everyone.

11. **Power Surge** 5.10 A

12. **Stiff Fingers** 5.9
Obscure route 30 ft. right of the above climb.

Boulders in the Woods

1. **The T. Tube** 5.9

2. **Burgerville** 5.10 C

3. **Kindergarten Snack** 5.2

Breakfast Cracks

This small but historical amphitheatre offers several of the finest 5.10 cracks at the Butte.

1. **"D" and Rising** 5.10 B

2. **The Arete** 5.12A
3 QD's and #2 Friend
A bolted arete at the left corner of this little amphitheatre. Looks climbable but not easily clippable.

3. **Blackberry Jam** 5.10 B ★★★
Pro to 2"
Very popular local favorite at the Butte. A steep crack system ending with a stiff crux exit move.

4. **Hot Tang** 5.10 C (variation)

A quick fingertips start to Blackberry Jam. Interesting.

5. **Expresso** 5.9 ★★
Pro to 2"
An obvious dihedral corner with a dirty exit move. Fun and quite popular. Climb the right facing corner.

6. **Red Zinger** 5.11 C ★★
Pro to 1"
An excellent and difficult undercling smear problem. Frequently top-roped and good for a quick pump. Start as per Expresso, but attack the seam that diagonals up right to a brushy slope.

7. **Orange Spice** 5.11 B ★
A top-rope face problem that ascends vertical rock diagonally to join with Lemon Twist. A good but short climb.

8. **Lemon Twist** (Direct Start) 5.10 B

9. **Lunge and Plunge** 5.11 (TR)

10. **White Rabbit** 5.10 B ★★★
Pro to 1"
One of the original all time favorites at Rocky Butte. Commence up right to a crack, then follow this up leftward then directly to the top of the cliff. Eases at about two-thirds height to sloping steps then a final vertical move.

11. **White Rabbit Buttress** 5.11+ ★★
An exciting climb ascending the outside face just to the right of White Rabbit. Start up thin holds just to the right of White Rabbit to several good large holds, then move up on sidepulls and clings until possible to move up lef onto the slabs above. Continue to top.

12. **Unknown** 5.12 C (TR)

13. **Harder Than Life** 5.11 D (TR)

14. **Bird of Paradise** 5.10 D ★★★
Pro to 2"
A very popular, well deserving classic at Rocky Butte. One of the best. Start by angling up easy steps to a stance next to a fir tree (or by starting directly up a dihedral 20 ft. below the tree and hidden from view), then climb the crack on the left of the tree. Undercling through the crux and jam upward to the top of the crag.

15. _____ 5.12 (TR)

16. **Wisdom Tooth** 5.11 B

17. _____ 5.10
Prominent dihedral that diagonals up leftwardto the summit. 100 ft. long.

18. **Trix are for Kids** 5.11+ (TR)
A beautiful, difficult overhang seam face climb partway up the same prominent dihedral. Step onto the right face at 1/2 height to ascend.

19. **Time of Your Life** 5.11 A (TR)
An excellent arete problem that starts up the aforementioned dihedral.

Breakfast Cracks

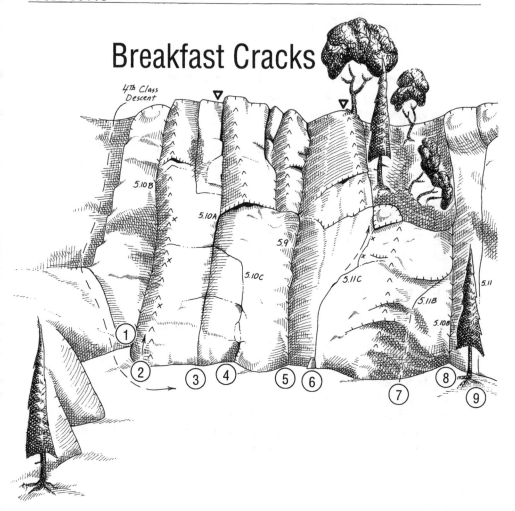

Traverse to the arete near a patch of bright yellow lichen. Ascend via the left then right side of the arete.

20. **Swiss Miss** 5.10 B
Pro to 2 1/2" TCU's recommended
A crack that leads to the right side of the same arete. Makes use of natural pockets for protection. TCUs a must. Crux is a minor bulge 25 ft. up and may need pins.

Wall of Shadows

As the cliff curves west from Breakfast Cracks you will find the secluded Wall of Shadows and beyond is The Grotto. New housing development limits use in this area.

1. **Shadows in Space** 5.10 B
2. **Face Disgrace** 5.11+ variation
3. **Skywalker** 5.10 D
4. **Mystic Traveler** 5.11 (R)
5. **Spider Line** 5.11+
6. **Foot Loose** 5.9
7. **Joe's Garden** 5.6
8. **Hang Loose** 5.11+ (TR)
9. **Seventh Wave** 5.12 A

Carver Bridge Cliff

The fabulous and elusive Carver Bridge Cliff. For generations this small crag remained well hidden under thick carpets of moss and vegetation.
Though nearly impenetrable, early "pioneers" did venture to Carver to climb on this hidden crag. The occasional fixed piton attested to this fact. Even on the Yellow Wall (on Angular Motion) there was an old fixed 10 ft. rope hanging from a bashie, ascended in 1975 by Jeff Alzner and Terry Jenkins.

Late in the summer of 1987, several climber's visited here and immediately realized its vast potential for free climbing routes. In a few short years, incredible amounts of vegetation were removed to produce a local climber's paradise. The super classics are numerous and the climbing here is indeed excellent.

The Carver Bridge Cliff formation extends roughly along an east-west axis for several hundred yards in length. Minor outcrops do occur beyond the main sections described, but are not developed for climbing. The highest portion of the cliff (Rockgarden Wall) is approximately 130 ft. tall. Carver has four sections of wall that have been named and developed for climbing purposes. They are as follows: the Rockgarden Wall, the Wall In-Between, Yellow Wall and Ivy League Buttress. The majority of the routes are rated from 5.9 to 5.12 and most are bolted or pinned. In other words, you may have to look hard to find an "R" rated climb at Carver.

Greg Lyon, Mike Pajunas, Robert McGown, Gary Rall, Wayne Wallace and others were highly instrumental in the development of this crag.

Here are several astounding classics to test your fingertips: **Smerk** (5.11 A), **Angular Motion** (5.12 A), **Uncola** (5.11 C), **Notorious** (5.11 B), **Sea of Holes** (5.12 A) and **Rites of Passage** (5.10 B - first pitch). These and a host of other great climbs helped to set the area on edge and in motion.

There are also many bouldering problems located in the woods below the main crag. As of this printing many of the upper climbing routes, the In Between Wall, as well as some of the climbs at the west end are heavily vegetated and unusable. Yet, the better climbs are quite climbable and are still a challenge.

Carver is a very small crag under private ownership. Continued freedom of access ultimately depends upon your willingness to obey the rules.

The following guidelines apply to all visitors who visit Carver Bridge Cliff. It is privately owned. To gain access you must sign a liability release waiver, obtainable at the Portland Rock Gym. When visiting the crag you must carry photo I.D. as well as Carver Climbing Club identification. Do not litter, or vandalize, no excessive noise, respect *all* rights of the owner, including right of privacy, and be vigilant concerning others who may trespass or cause problems that may jeopardize access privileges. Only club members are allowed.

Rockgarden Wall

1. **Crack in the Mirror** 5.9 ★★
   30' Pro to 1 1/2"
   At the far left side of the wall and just uphill is a unique looking 'broken' flake start. Ascend this and exit right to an anchor at a ledge.

2. _____ 5.10 A (variation)
   15' Pro unknown

3. **Notorious** 5.11 C/D ★★★
   35' 5 QD's
   One of the great Carver classics. A very good climb! Climb the arete via large holds to a ledge and finish up left to an anchor.

4. **Margueritaville** 5.10 D
   40' Pro to 2"
   The deep overhung dihedral. A stiff crux. Join with Uncola.

5. **Cherry Cola** 5.11 D (variation) ★★

Greg Lyon cruising Angular Motion (5.12 A)

73

25' 4 QD's

This difficult problem begins off the top of a large boulder and joins with Uncola before ending at the bolt anchor.

6. **Uncola** 5.11 C ★★★

45' 5 QD's

One of the ten great Carver classics. Located just left of a large chimney. Move up to the top of the boulder, step right onto the face. Ascend the wild, slightly overhung, awkward face up left past a harsh crux. Bolt belay. An excellent route!

7. **Neptune** 5.9 ★★

40' Pro to 1 1/2"

The obvious wide offwidth. A fun climb. Stem, jam and body climb up to a bolt belay. A minor crack on the right face of the chimney offers good small pro.

8. **Smooth Torquer** 5.12 C/D ★★

45' 4 QD's

An excellent, desperate, physical "tips" climb just to the left of Smerk. Eases to a smooth slab after the crux. Bolt anchor.

9. **Smerk** 5.11 A ★★★

120' (40' 1st pitch) Pro = QD's

One of the finest classic routes at Carver Bridge Cliff. Very popular! Ascend a bolted face left of New Generation past a crux (5.11 A) exiting to the belay on the right. The second pitch (4 bolts) ascends directly up the headwall (5.10 C) to another bolt anchor. The third pitch finishes straight up a smooth face (2 bolts) via a diagonal seam start. Bolt belay.

10. **New Generation** 5.9+ ★★★

120' (40' 1st pitch) Pro to 1 1/2"

A popular climb. Begin up an awkward start to a small corner and climb a sweet finger crack (5.8) to a bolt belay. Angle up left via a low angle ramp to another bolted face. Continue up this (5.9+) to a ledge, then finish up an arete (5.9) to a fir tree belay. Rappel or walk off.

11. **Free Ride** 5.12 A (variation)

15' 2 QD's

A bolted direct start to Scotch and Soda.

12. **Scotch and Soda** 5.10 D ★★★

40' QD's and pro to 1 1/2"

Fantastic crack and face climb. Start at a ledge beneath the Red Dihedral. Ascend a harsh finger crack until possible to maneuver left onto a small pedestal. Finish up a bolted face to an anchor.

13. **Tequila Sunrise** 5.10 C

120' Pro to 2"

Start as for Scotch and Soda, but traverse right to Red Dihedral, then up left around a minor corner to the New Generation anchor. Continue up easy ramps to the left then up and right (1 bolt) through a 5.10 A crux to a ledge. Move up a 5.8 crack and offwidth to the summit. Bolt belay.

14. **Red Dihedral** 5.10 A ★★
60' Pro to 1 1/2" TCU's recommended
Interesting dihedral. Originally named due to the red lichen on the rock. Pull up a crux start into the corner and ascend this up and then right to a stubby maple tree. Move past this and up a tight crux corner to a large ledge and bolt anchor on the right.

15. _____ 5.12 +
60' (TR)

16. **Jungle Safari** 5.10 A ★★
120' Pro to 3"
An excellent LONG dihedral climb. Begin just left of the offwidth (Combination Block) and stem, jam your way up an awkward corner. The crux is a narrow section 80 ft. up. Finish up a steep but easy (5.8) fist crack to a tree belay.

17. **Night Vision** 5.11 B ★★
120' (65' 1st pitch) Pro to 1 1/2"
Not often climbed because it requires some pro, but is a superb route nonetheless. Commence up the offwidth crack on the left side of Combination Block. Follow a minor corner up and over a wild bulge then up a stiff face (crux) to a bolt anchor. The next pitch ascends a 5.9 crack up right to the top of the cliff.

18. **Sanity Assassin** 5.7 to 5.10
20' 2 QD's

19. **Sea of Holes** 5.12 A ★★★
75' 7 QD's
A beautiful classic and one of the finest at Carver. Begin from off the top of Combination Block and ascend the rounded buttress (crux) via unique pocketed face holds and edges. Enter a shallow dihedral where the route eases. Exit up right to a bolt belay.

⊗. **Sport Court** 5.12 C ★★★
75' 8 QD's
This exciting superior route exists by connecting the lower half of Sea of Holes with the upper half of Wally Street.

20. **Shadowfox** 5.8 ★
25' Pro to 3/4"
A short crack climb on a smooth slab. A good approach to the upper face climbs.

21. **Wally Street** 5.12 A ★★★
70' 5 QD's and minor pro to 3/4"
Start as for Shadowfox but enter up left onto a stiff, vertical face climb of quality proportion.

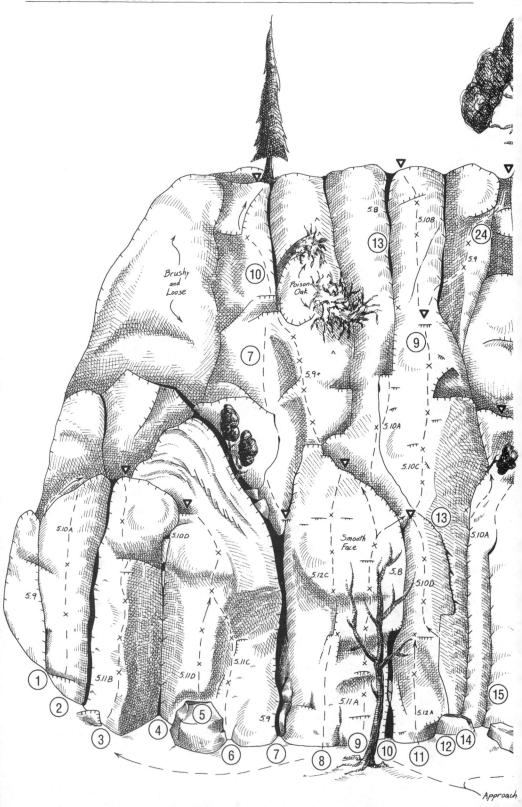

Rockgarden Wall

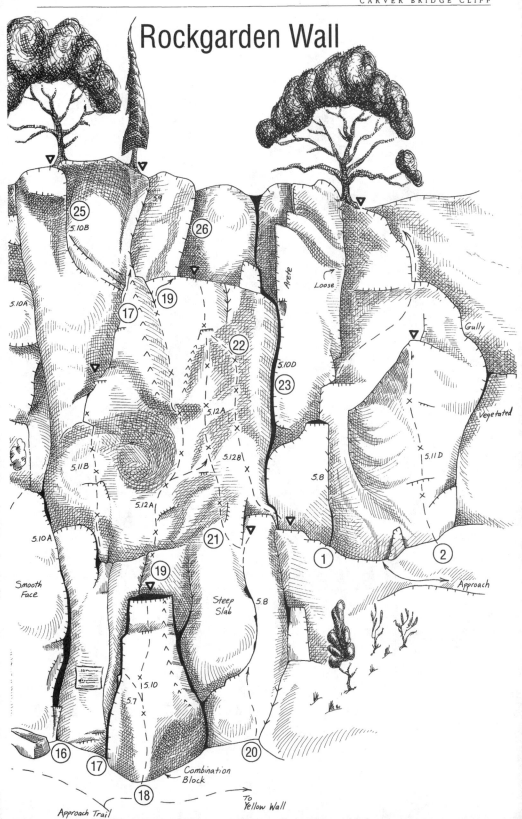

5.10B — 25

5.9

26

5.10A

17

19

22

5.10D

23

Arete

Loose

Gully

Vegetated

5.11B

5.12A

5.12B

5.12A

5.11D

5.8

5.10A

Smooth Face

21

1

2

Approach

19

Steep Slab

5.8

5.10

5.7

16

17

20

18

Combination Block

To Yellow Wall

Approach Trail

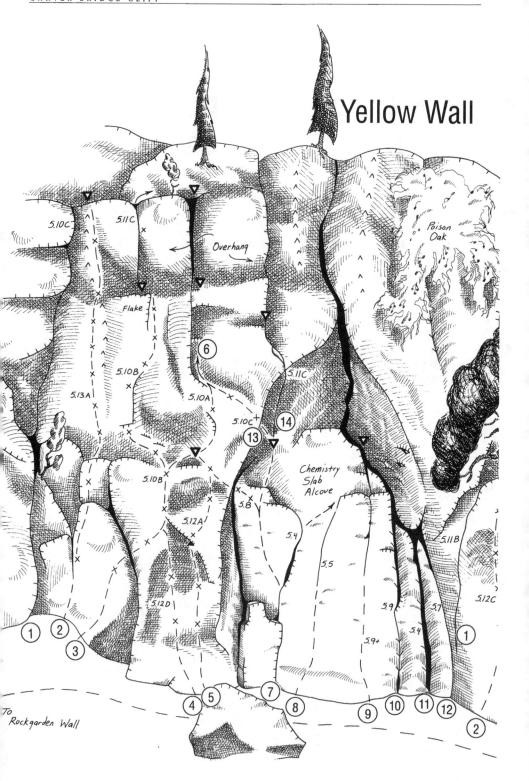

Yellow Wall

5.10C

5.11C

Overhang

Flake

⑥

5.10B

5.13A

5.10A

5.10C

⑭

⑬

5.11C

Chemistry
Slab
Alcove

5.10B

5.8

5.12A

5.4

5.5

5.12D

5.9

5.7

5.11B

5.12C

①

②

③

⑤

④

⑦

⑧

5.9+

5.4

⑨

⑩

⑪

⑫

①

②

Poison
Oak

To
Rockgarden Wall

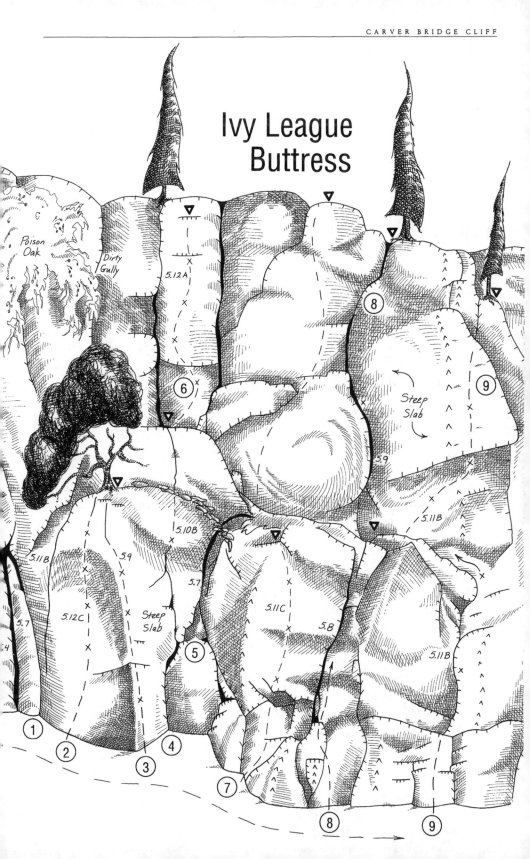

Ivy League Buttress

Poison
Oak

Dirty
Gully

5.12A

⑥

⑧

Steep
Slab

⑨

5.9

5.11B

5.10B

5.9

5.11B

5.7

Steep
Slab

5.11C

5.8

5.12C

⑤

5.11B

5.7

4

①

②

③

④

⑦

⑧

⑨

22. **Wally Wedding** 5.12 B
20' 4 QD's

23. **Sweat and the Flies** 5.10 D
20' Pro to 3"
This bold flared offwidth is a surprising lead. Short and nasty, designed to
dare anyone.

24. **Battleship Arete** 5.9 (variation)
20' 2 QD's

25. **Night Life** 5.10 B
35' Pro to 1 1/2"

26. **Holiday in Cambodia** 5.10 A
20' (TR)

Wall In-Between

1. **Passport to Insanity** 5.8
35' Pro to 2"
Ascend a perfect corner, mantle to a ledge, then mantle again, continuing
up right, then left to an oak tree belay.

2. **Burning From the Inside** 5.11 D ★★
20' 3 QD's
This exhilarating problem dances up an overhung rounded face to a bolt
belay. A great climb.

3. **Hinge of Fate** 5.10 C
25' 3 QD's and optional pro to 3/4"
At the top of a dirt gully you will find a dark, water streaked face. Ascend
this past a crux, then lay back and smear your way up a flared seam (the
hinge).

4. **Eyes of a Stranger** 5.10 A
40' Pro to 3/4"

5. **Shady Personality** 5.10 B
65' Pro to 1 1/2" Cams recommended
A unique climb that can be done in two short pitches. Move up a smooth
slab (5.9) and up easy steps to a belay on a ledge. Continue up a slightly
overhung crack that begins as a mantle into an offwidth pea-pod. Bolt
belay.

6. **Rats in the Jungle** 5.10 A
20' Wide pro to 6"
The large chimney problem immediately right of Shady Personality.

Yellow Wall

1. **Call to Greatness** 5.10 C ★★

60' Pro to 2"

An impressive route. Classic thin hand jamming. Begin up a large brushing corner at the left edge of the Yellow Wall. Embark from a stance up the overhung crack system. Boldly climb around three small bulges, the hardest being the last. The main distraction is the Plastic Monkey anchor affixed to the wall at the crux exit move.

2. **Plastic Monkey** 5.13 A

60' 7 QD's

A very difficult problem and one of the hardest at Carver. Ascend the vertical bolted face on the left corner of the Yellow Wall.

3. **Rites of Passage** 5.11 C   ★★★

80' 10 QD's

One of the finest, most popular routes at the crag. Commence up a face (1 bolt) and move right (or start up a jam crack to this point), then up a bolted face (5.10 B) until possible to move right to an anchor above Angular Motion. Step back left and continue up via a shallow corner (5.10 B) then up right to a flake to another bolt anchor just under an overhang. Rappel or charge up the thin crack above (1 bolt and pro to 1") leading to the summit.

4. **Digital** 5.12 D ★★

20' 4 QD's

A unique, yet difficult balance problem.

5. **Angular Motion** 5.12 A ★★★

40' 5 QD's

One of the most popular climbs here. Super classic! To the left of Chemistry Slab is an overhung face. Power your way up this until you must make a long reach to a jug then up right on tenuous holds to a ledge and a bolt belay. An exciting route with dynamic moves.

6. **Out on a Limb** 5.10 A ★

60' QD's and pro to 1 1/2"

A good route. Start up the left side of Chemistry Slab alcove. Exit out left along a narrow ramp (crux) and up to a bolt anchor. Belay, then continue up a face (1 bolt) that leads to a dihedral above. Rappel from a bolt anchor under the final overhang.

The next six climbs are easy problems on the Chemistry Slab.

7. **Smooth Operator** 5.4 ★

40' Pro to 1 1/2"

8. **Talent Show** 5.5 ★

40' Pro to 3/4" TCU's and small wires

9. **Blue Monday** 5.9+ ★

40' (TR)

10. **Crimson Tide** 5.9 ★
    40' Pro to 2"

11. **Spearfishing in Bermuda** 5.4
    40' Large pro

12. **Leaning Uncertainty** 5.7
    15' Pro to 2"

13. **King Rat** 5.10 C
    60' Pro to 1 1/2"
    An 'out on a limb' route that exits the upper left side of Chemistry Slab alcove.

14. **Chariots of Fire** 5.11 C ★★★
    55' Pro to 2"
    An incredible and physical climb. A Carver classic for sure. Race up easy slabs passing a bolt anchor. Enter a hand jam crack leading directly up a desperately overhung wall. Exit past a block to a bolt anchor on a small ledge.

Ivy League Buttress

1. **Dreamscape** 5.11 B ★★
    30' Pro to 1 1/2"
    A beautiful tips crack that breaks the right outer face of Chemistry alcove. Ends at the maple tree belay.

2. **Rip Grip** 5.12 C ★★
    30' 4 QD's
    A bolted face immediately right of Dreamscape.

3. **Rubicon** 5.9 ★★
    30' 3 QD's and minor pro to 3/4"
    A very popular easy climb for everyone. Ascend the outside corner to easy edges, then up a steep face (crux) until you can grab the base edge of a thin crack. Tree belay.

4. **Edge of the Reef** 5.10 B ★★
    45' Pro to 1" TCU's recommended
    A really good climb. Challenging but not extreme. Move up the curved starting crack (numerous edges) then straight up a crack past a face crux with 1 bolt. Finish up a thin crack that rounds to a slab and bolt anchor.

5. **Great Barrier Reef** 5.7 (R)
    30' Pro unknown

6. **Penguins in Heat** 5.12 A
    30' 4 QD's
    A difficult problem located above the first pitch of Edge of the Reef.

7. **Challenger** 5.11 B/C ★★
    30' 3 QD's TCU's optional

The name describes the route very well. This quality climb begins up easy steps until you must enter a smooth face broken with unusual edges. Finish up and left to exit at a bolt anchor.

8. **Last of the Mohicans** 5.9 ★
   40' Pro to 2 1/2"
   A good, enjoyable climb to learn the basics. Ascend a broken crack system with a bulge on the right side just short of the anchor.

9. **Riders of the Purple Sage** 5.10 B
   40' QD's and pro to 1"
   Step up easy ground to a considerably overhung corner (1 bolt). Stem and layback up right then left to the bolt anchor. Rappel.

Beacon Rock

Climbers could not have asked for a finer big wall crag than Beacon Rock. This is the place! Technically demanding, sustained dihedral rock climbing of the finest degree can be found here on the huge 400' vertical south face.

Beacon has enchanted and hauntingly enticed generations of adventurers even before the first ascent of the **SE Face** in April of 1954 by John Ohrenschall and Gene Todd. The name of this historical monument of rock was coined by the Lewis and Clark expedition of 1805-1806. It stood as a final "beacon" to these early explorers of the Oregon Country. In 1915 Henry J. Biddle initiated the building of the present day trail which leads to the summit of the rock. In 1935 the rock was established as part of the Washington State Park System, so that all could enjoy the beauty and wonder of this majestic monolith.

In 1961 the early roots of rock climbing at Beacon had begun. The spectacular efforts of Eugene Dod, Bob Martin, and Earl Levin came true when they succeeded in ascending a prominent crack and offwidth system to Big Ledge. To this day **Dod's Jam** (5.10 C) stands as a remarkable and classic example of early route pioneering achievement.

Throughout the latter half of the 1960's an inner core of climbers broke major barriers via mixed free and aid climbing technique. They created instant attractions like **Flying Swallow** (5.10 D), **Right** and **Left Gull** (5.10 A), **Jensen's Ridge** (5.11 B), culminating with a ascent of **Blownout** (5.10 A) in January 1969 by Steve Strauch and Danny Gates. Dean Caldwell, Dave Jensen, Steve Strauch, Kim Schmitz, Bob Martin and others involved in the scene will long be remembered for their efforts.

The next decade provided an even wider variety of mixed free and aid ascents. Two such notable feats certainly would have to be Les Nugent's ascent of **Steppenwolf** (5.10 D) and **Free For All** (5.8) in 1973 by Dean Fry and Steve Lyford. The mid 1970's brought a new group of climbers to the crag as they ascended superb routes like **Flight Time** (5.11 C), **Pipeline** (5.11 A), **Blood, Sweat and Smears** (5.10 C) and **Free For Some** (5.11 A). Jeff Thomas, Mark Cartier, Ted Johnson, Avery Tichner, Alan Kearney, Jim Olson, Mike Smelsar, Robert McGown and others frequently turned toward the countless old aid lines, discovering that these routes produced excellent free climbs. Free climbing was now vogue.

The following decades have continued to bring an even wider spectrum of climbers to Beacon. From this new generation of climbers came quality routes like **Cruisin'** (5.7), **Fear of Flying** (5.10 B), **Bladerunner** (5.10 C), **Winter Delight** (5.10 B), **Borderline** (5.11 B), **Excalibur** (5.12 B), **Flying Dutchman** (5.10 B) and **Windsurfer** (5.10 B). Those who continued to test the edge in the

1980's and 1990's were mainly Ron Allen, Scott Tracy, Mark Cartier, Darryl Nakahira, Jim Opdycke, Robert McGown, Wayne Wallace, Nathan Charleton and Jim Yoder. Uncountable tales have yet to be told in the years to come, as only time will tell. So stay tuned to Beacon Rock.

Beacon Rock is a part of the Washington State Park System. The following park rules are to be observed while climbing here.

Climbing is presently limited to the river or south face. The south face is closed from February 1 until approximately July 15 due to Peregrine Falcon nesting. Portions of the east face of Beacon Rock are tentatively planned for opening in the summer of 2001 and this will add tremendously to climbing options. The Northwest area of Beacon Rock *is* open year-round and presently offers about twelve rock climbs.

The park discourages climbers from parking in the boat ramp and camping area west of Beacon Rock. The amount of space for automobiles is limited and the railroad company does not like climbers walking along its tracks.

Any violation of the rules would jeopardize the privilege of climbing on Beacon Rock. Check with the park manager for further updated information.

There are several objective dangers while climbing on the south face of Beacon Rock: poison oak and rockfall. Rockfall is generated from above near the west side hikers' trail at a point above the third tunnel where sightseers gather. Above the Southeast Face route climbers occasionally stir up trouble when dragging the rope through loose rocks on Grassy Ledges. Occasional accidents and countless close calls due to stonefall have occurred. Because there is a risk of encountering rockfall while at the base of the cliff climbing helmets are recommended for personal safety. If other people are known to be climbing above you on the Southeast Face or Right Gull, take extra precaution. The other problem is poison oak. Usually, long pants will suffice. Learn to recognize the three-leaf pattern and color. Some of the climbing routes up left of the Arena of Terror are virtually unclimbable because of the oak. Take the necessary precautions and learn to avoid both.

When climbing at Beacon Rock competency is a must! Climbing here is not for beginners nor to learn basic skills. Many of the routes are multi-pitch and quite challenging while the scenery in the Columbia Gorge is superb, all good reasons to visit Beacon Rock.

The directions are as follows. Beacon Rock is 28.8 miles east of Portland from I-205 on the Washington side of the Columbia River. Drive east from Vancouver on State 14 from 30 minutes, or east on I-84 to Bridge of the Gods, then west on State 14 to this famous andesitic monolith of the Gorge.

Climb safely and enjoy your stay.

The following routes are described from right to left and begin near where the east side hikers trail meets the base of the southeast buttress. The great forboding east face, with its spectrum of secret routes, lies just to the right.

1. **Pacific Rim** II 5.10 C ★★
   Multi-pitch   QD's and minor pro to 1"
   A fantastic route that will keep you on the edge all the way. Begin under the well protected overhangs (of the east face) twenty feet downhill and left of a large alcove. Commence up a shallow corner then face climb (bolts) up right along the virtual edge of the abyss directly below. Belay at a 2 bolt anchor. Rappel 60' or continue up right (bolts) until you can climb a vertical corner that eases to a dihedral. Bolt belay up right on a ledge. Rappel with two ropes 120'. The upper headwall has yet to be completed, yet holds excellent promise.

2. **Boardwalk** 5.6
   Pro to 2" Two rope rappel (120')
   A long, obvious right facing dihedral approx. 40' uphill from the trail. Climb the corner up to a roof, step right then up to a bolt anchor.

3. **Young Warriors** III 5.9 ★★
   This 5 pitch route begins left of Boardwalk, and ascends in a direct line via crack corner systems passing Tree Ledge on the right.

5. **Obnoxious Cubbyhole** 5.7 A2
   Nail up to the right of Stone Rodeo until the two routes meet at the large roof. Not recommended.

6. **Stone Rodeo** 5.12 A ★★★
   65' QD's and minor pro to 3"   Friends recommended
   A supreme example of physical endurance. As the hikers' trail meets the cliff beneath Cruisin', look to the right 25 ft. past an oak tree. Beyond is a bolted overhung face that leads up through a roof split with a crack. Climb this and enjoy. Excellent rock. Pro needed for roof.

7. **Rock Police** II 5.10 C ★
   QD's and pro to 1" TCU's required   Poor hangers
   To the right of the same oak tree 15 ft. is a bolted face that follows a right leaning arete. Unusual climb but still fun. Poor hangers. Climb up a face (to the left of Stone Rodeo) to a bulge crux move (bolt). Angle up right on a steep slab staying near the arete (crux), eventually easing to a ledge and bolt anchor. Rappel 65 ft. or angle up left to the second belay on the SE Face route. From there move up right (5.9) to a slabby right-facing arete. Rejoins with SE Face near the top of the slab.

8. **Return to the Sky** 5.10 A
   65' Pro to 1 1/2"
   A seldom climbed route that angles over several dihedrals then up a corner. Start behind the oak tree and climb up right past a bolt (crux) then upward to a bolt belay. Rappel.

9. **Sky Pilot** 5.11 A
   95' Pro to 2"
   Start as for Return To The Sky except storm through a weakness in the overhang above. Obscure.

10. **Couchmaster** 5.9
    100' Pro to 1 1/2"
    Start up slab behind oak tree, step left and turn corner stemming up (crux)
    to join with Cruisin'.

11. **Jingus Jam** 5.9 (variation)
    35' Pro to 2"

12. **Cruisin' Direct Finish** 5.11 C (variation)
    25' Pro to 3/4" Needs pitons

13. **Cosmic Dust** 5.10 B (variation)
    25' Pro to 1"

14. **Cruisin'** (a.k.a. Cruisemaster) 5.7 ★★★
    100' Pro to 2"
    An excellent local favorite. And rightly so. Start up a fun slab 15 ft. left of
    the large oak tree. Follow a thin crack (crux) to an overhang. Move left
    to sidestep the roof, then continue up a dihedral to easy ledges. Belay at
    the established anchors on the SE Face.

15. **Stardust** 5.8 ★
    100' Pro to 1 1/2"
    Start up a left facing corner to a small roof. Turn this by sidesteping
    around to the right and continue up until it joins Cruisin'.

16. **Rock Master** 5.11 C ★★
    100' Pro to 2" TCU's required
    Technically very bold. Stem up a left facing corner (crux) using very
    unorthodox maneuvers to succeed (#0 TCU). Pull through a difficult roof
    move and up a crack system that eases and joins with the SE Face route.

17. **Rookie Nookie** 5.10 C ★★
    100' Pro to 2"
    Slightly uphill and left of Rock Master is a prominent left-facing dihedral
    with one fixed piton. A great climb. Joins with the SE Face route.

18. **Icy Treats** (a.k.a. Frozen Treats) 5.10 D (R) ★
    100' Pro to 1 1/2" Needs more fixed gear.
    Look for a shallow corner with two bolts near the start. A difficult stem
    problem with hard to place pro and a little runout in places. Climb up
    past the bolts to a halfway stance. More awkward, desperate smears lead
    to the top where it joins the SE Face route.

19. **Switchblade** 5.11 A
    110' Pro unknown

20. **Bladerunner** 5.10 C ★★
    110' Pro to 2"
    An incredible route and an excellent prize. Begin up and pull through (1
    bolt) a loose section of rock to a stance. Angle up left then straight up a
    seam (2 bolts and crux) until the crack widens and eases in difficulty.
    Belay at bolts just below Snag Ledge tree.

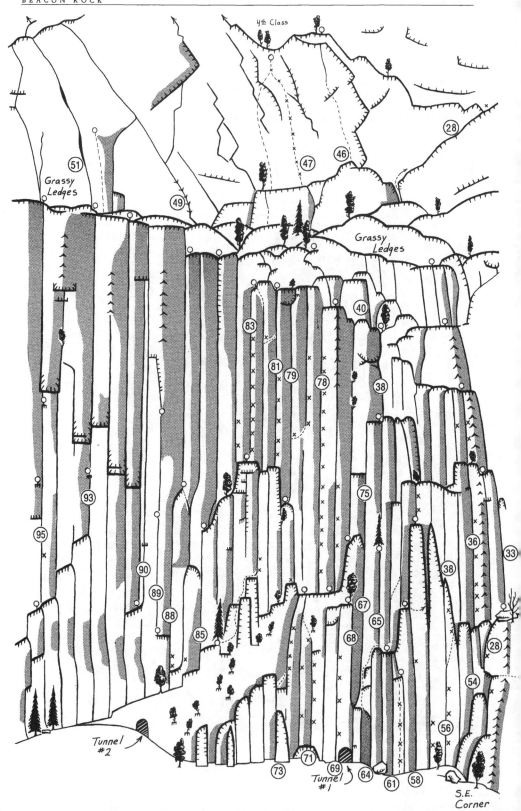

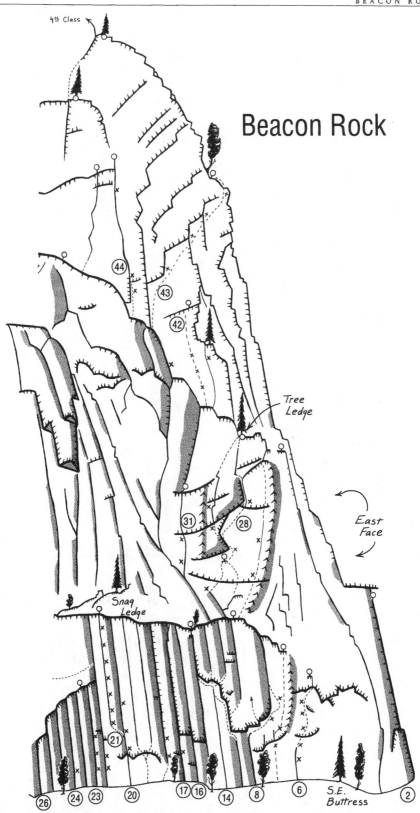

4th Class

Beacon Rock

Tree
Ledge

East
Face

Snag
Ledge

S.E.
Buttress

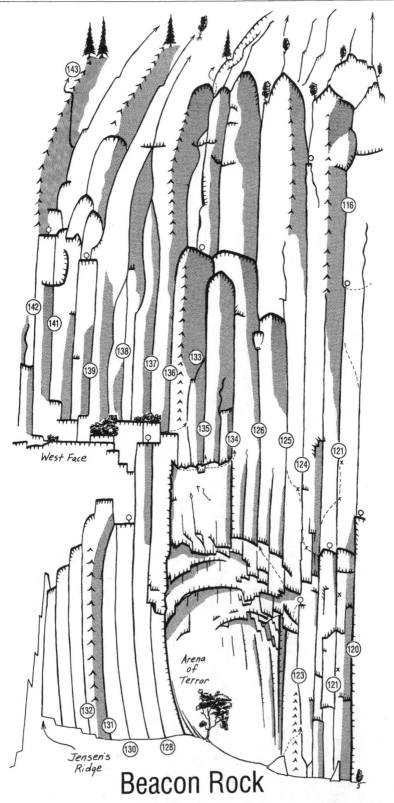

West Face

Arena
of
Terror

Jensen's
Ridge

Beacon Rock

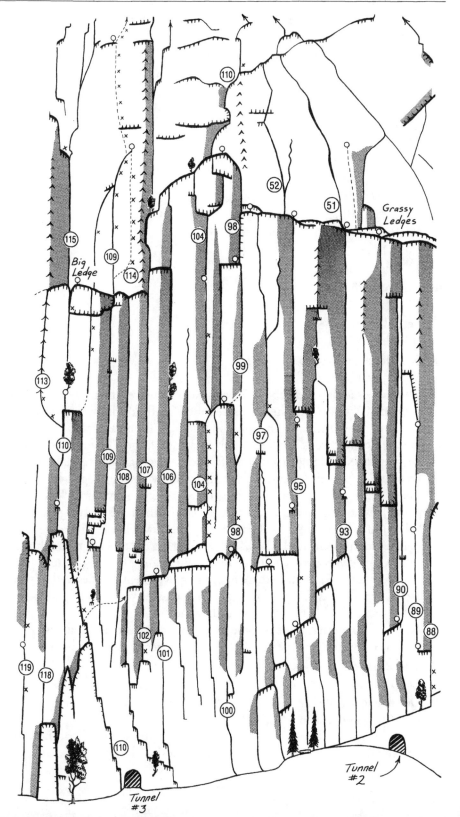

21. **Fire and Ice** 5.11 B ★★★
   110' QD's, small wires, and TCU's to 1"
   A demanding, exciting and high quality classic. A modern climb on the smooth, rounded arete slab left of Bladerunner. Climb up Bladerunner to the second bolt, traverse left onto the face and go straight up the bolt line. From a stance above the halfway crux, step left to finish up a thin seam (pitons) which ends at the Snag Ledge tree.

22. **More Balls Than Nuts** 5.11 B (R)
   50' Thin pro to 1"

23. **No Balls, No Falls** 5.11 A
   50' QD's and pro to 1"

24. **Levitation Blues** 5.10 D
   50' QD's and pro to 1"

25. **Repo Man** 5.10 C
   40' Pro to 1"

26. **Cigarette** 5.10 A
   30' Pro to 1"

26. **Lethal Ejection** 5.9
   60' Pro to 2"

28. **Southeast Face** III 5.7 ★★★
   Multi-pitch Pro to 2"
   The first established climb on Beacon Rock. Interesting route that meanders up 600' of rock to the west side hikers' trail. Begin west and uphill of a prominent corner near the railroad tracks. Climb easy steps (2 fixed pitons) on clean rock 80 ft. to a bolt belay at a ledge. Traverse horizontally right (NE) along ledges 70 ft. to another bolt anchor. Belay. Move up a slab to the left (or surmount bulge directly above), step right (crux), then up around a roof and continue up a slab corner system. When possible work rightward to turn an exposed corner (SE Buttress directly below) then up to the Tree Ledge belay. Follow a left leaning dihedral ramp system to Grassy Ledges. Belay. Wander up and left through a short off-width move. Continue up a right leaning low angle ramp (1/4" bolt near top). Exit left here along small grassy steps, bushes and 4th class ground until it eases. Or move right to a tree belay, then straight up to a notch and scramble into the woods beyond.
   Note: be aware that there is loose rock on Grassy Ledges. It is easily disturbed by foot or rope and is a serious danger to climbers below.

29. **Variation** 5.9
   25' Pro to 2"

30. **Desdichado** 5.10 C
   40' QD's and pro to 1 1/2"
   A unique short climb with poor hangers. Located about 1/3 of the way up the crux pitch of the Southeast Face on a slightly overhung corner.

31. **Dynaflux** 5.11 B
50' QD's and pro to 1 1/2"
Up left from the second belay on the Southeast Face is a bulging face with
a vertical crack in it. Two bolts protect the hardest moves. Rappel from
bolt anchor.

32. _____

33. **Jill's Thrill** 5.9
160' (2 80' leads) Pro to 2"
A fun route, especially the second half. Start at Snag Ledge belay. Move
up to and climb a minor corner with 2 fixed pitons. Belay at anchor on a
ledge to the left at 70 ft. Step back right and continue up a flared slabby
crack system 70 ft. to a large gravelly ledge and bolt anchor. Rappel.
Note: This is one of the established 80 ft. rappels on Beacon Rock from
Grassy Ledges. There are many rappels, but this one is less exposed and
conveniently oriented near the SE Face.

34. **Tooth Faerie**
5.10 A
70' Pro to 2"
#0 TCU recom-
mended
Ascend a clean
crack directly
above belay
anchor. At the
flakey overhang
face climb up the
left side of crack to
join with Jill's
Thrill.

35. **To the Edge and
Beyond** 5.11 B
70' Pro to 2"
including TCU's
Somewhat con-
trived, but chal-
lenging.

36. **Fear of Flying**
5.10 B ★★★
160' Pro to 1 1/2"
A superb Beacon
Rock climb. Step
left from the Snag
Ledge belay and
commence up a

Cindy Olson climbing Winter Delight (5.10B)

dihedral protected with 4 fixed pins. From a belay ledge at 65 ft. continue up a thin crack (2 pitons) until possible to step right and join Jill's Thrill.

37. **Desperado** 5.10 D (R)
160' Thin pro to 1 1/2" and pitons

38. **Right Gull** III 5.10 A (or 5.7 A0) ★★★
Multi-pitch Pro to 3"
A very popular route with plenty of variety. From the Snag Ledge belay step left around a corner and enter a large right-facing corner. Climb this until it tops out on a pedestal, then gingerly move left to a bolt anchor. Either A0 or free climb (5.10 A crux) past 2 fixed pitons to a ledge. Above are several options. On the right is an offwidth (4"); in the center, a slightly dirty left leaning crack; or on your left is a fist crack (3"). All of these are approx. 5.8. At the top of these options, step left to a bolt anchor on a comfortable ledge. Bluebird and several other routes end here as well. Continue up a wide crack pulling through an awkward bulge to a rocky ledge with a small oak tree. Wander up behind the tree and left-ward via a series of steps to another bolt anchor and Grassy Ledges.

39. **Vulcan's Variation** 5.8
12' Pro to 3/4"
A rather convenient way to bypass the crux on Right Gull. Climb a thin crack to the right of the second belay and above a sharp ear of rock.

40. **Muriel's Memoir** 5.9
25' Pro to 1 1/2"
When Right Gull eases to the rocky ledge near a small oak tree, look to your left. This is the good looking clean corner crack. Rejoins with regular route.

The following 13 routes are located above Grassy Ledges beginning near Tree Ledge and ending at Flying Swallow.

41. **Synapse** 5.10 C 35' Pro to 1"

42. **Death and Taxes** 5.12 C ★★
45' QD's and minor pro to 1"
This short, premium quality face climb utilizes a series of incipient seams and edges. A very unusual climb to be found here at Beacon. It is located approximately 40 ft. up and left of Tree Ledge (SE Face route).

43. **Lost Variation** II 5.8
Pro unknown
An indisputable route so named because numerous parties were unable to find it, yet it is rumored to be an interesting climb.

44. **Elusive Element** 5.10 D (R) ★
80' Pro to 1 1/2" including TCU's
A fabulous yet easily missed route roughly 100 ft. up left from Tree Ledge.

Lead up a right facing corner (crux) past 2 bolts to an easy slab. Continue up the crack to a short steep section (crux) and reach a bolt anchor just beyond. A really good climb except for the weird hangers and runout sections.

45. **Cloud Nine** 5.9
80' Pro to 2"
A bit mossy, but still a neat crack climb on a long slab. Located immediately uphill and left of Elusive Element. No fixed belay at present.

46. **High and Mighty** 5.11 B ★★
80' TCU's and wires to 1 1/2" Bolts or fixed pins needed
An excellent route high above Grassy Ledges. Located up left from the easy 5th class offwidth move on Grassy Ledges (SE Face route). Climb a wandering set of seams on a steep smooth face until possible to turn a corner leftward then up a crack on a slab. No fixed belay anchor.

47. **Sacrilege** 5.10 D ★★★
80' QD's and minor pro to 1"
A fantastic face climb on very steep terrain. Incredible lead and one of the few totally bolted Beacon classics. To the right of Diagonal Desperation is a large hidden terrace with an oak tree on it. This is the bolted route on the right side of the ledge.

48. _____ 5.12+
80 (TR)

49. **Diagonal Desperation** 5.10 D A0
Pro to 2" including pitons
Located just to the right of the upper pitches of Smooth Dancer. Climbs a left-leaning crack, then zig-zags before topping out.

50. _____

51. **Riverside** 5.10 B
Multipitch (80' 1st pitch) Pro to 2 1/2"
Probably one of the most unusual Beacon climbs available. Climbs a continuous and awkward flared left-leaning crack system near the left end of Grassy Ledges. Rappel after 80 ft. or continue to the west side trail.

52. _____ 5.11+
80' (TR)

Nathan Charleton on Excalibur (5.12B)

97

53. _____ 5.12+
    80' (TR)

The following routes are described right to left beginning immediately left of the SE Face route.

54. **Little Wing** 5.8 ★★
    80' Pro to 2"
    Immediately left of the SE Face route is a fun little classic climb that begins up easy slabby steps. Follow this and finish up a shallow well-protected corner until possible to step right at the Snag Ledge belay. The next pitch ascends a thin seam (5.10 B) above a small ledge directly above the first pitch. Joins with Fear of Flying.

55. **Broken Arrow** 5.10 A
    60' Pro to 1"

56. **Idiot** (a.k.a. Magester Ludi) 5.12 A
    120' QD's and pro to 1"
    Uphill and left of the SE Face is a smooth face with several thin climbs. The right is Idiot and the left is Magic Fingers. Ascend the difficult face (bolts and pitons) 40 ft. until you can reach over and use the outside corner of Right Gull. Layback up this (2 bolts) until necessary to join the Gull route.

57. **Magic Fingers** 5.12 C
    110' Pro to 2 1/2"
    This is the serious and demanding 2 bolt seam just left of the Idiot. Opens up to a large chimney on the last 25 ft. of Left Gull.

58. **Wrong Gull** II 5.10 C ★★
    110' Pro to 2 1/2"
    No two ways about it, a terrific climb with excellent pro. Start in the minor corner near an old tree stump. Stem up 80 ft. to a bolt anchor on a ledge. Then, if you're very bold, jam up the left side of a detached free standing pillar. Joins Right Gull.

59. **Sorcerer's Apprentice** 5.10 C
    40' Pro to 1"
    A thin seam crack immediately left of Wrong Gull.

60. **Old Warriors Never Die** 5.12 B ★
    80' QD's and minor pro to 1"
    A great bolted climb located on the outside of a minor rounded corner. Climb 45 ft. up the steep face and short dirty corner to a ledge. Belay at anchor. Rappel or continue up right (bolts) via dubious cracks to join with Wrong Gull at the bolt belay. Rappel.

61. **Seagull** II 5.10 C ★★★
    45' 1st pitch Pro to 1 1/2" Cams suggested
    This and the following climb are superb classics. They accurately portray

Beacon stem climbing at its finest. The route ascends a double cornered crack system (5.10 C) just to the right of a large boulder. Bolt belay on ledge (45'). Rappel or climb a thin crack above (5.10 D) to join with Right Gull. The first pitch is also known as **Ten-A-Cee Stemming**.

62. **Av's Route** 5.10 C ★★
45' Thin wires and pro to 1 1/2"
A fabulous route. Pure stemming on thin but good protection. Ascend the corner just left of the large boulder. Several fixed pitons after the crux. Beware of minor poison oak near the top of the climb.

63. **Too Close for Comfort** 5.12 A
This is the outside corner left of Av's Route.

64. **Left Gull** III 5.10 A or 5.8 A0
Multi-pitch Pro to 3"
An unusual but fun climb. Some poison oak and chimney climbing to contend with. Starts up broken corners and ledges immediately right of the first tunnel and joins with Right Gull at its second belay on the pedestal.

65. **Summer Daze** 5.11 C or C3 ★★
95' Thin wires and TCU's to 2 1/2"
Great climb with a desperate thin start. From the belay ledge at the top of Av's Route / Seagull step left then proceed up the seam (piton). The crack widens and passes a fir tree halfway up before it joins with Right Gull at a ledge belay.

66. _____ 5.12
130' (TR)
An outside arete and face between Summer Daze and Bluebird.

67. **Bluebird Direct** 5.10 D (R) ★
160' Pro to 2 1/2"
Directly above the first tunnel is a long dihedral. Commence up a thin seam on the tunnel's right side to a ledge 20 ft. up. Stem up a poorly protected dihedral to where it joins with the standard Bluebird route. A good climb but a little runout.

The following five routes offer high quality and only moderately difficult climbing. All are unique, several are serious but most are quite fun to lead.

68. **Spring Fever** 5.10 A ★★
55' Pro to 1 1/2"
Ascend the thin seam just to the right of the first tunnel. At the small ledge 20 ft. up step left and continue up a weird crack to a maple tree belay. Rappel.

69. **Winter Delight** 5.10 B ★★★
55' Pro to 1 1/2" (#2 TCU required)
A prize worth attaining and a delight to climb. Climbs a partly bolted

seam immediately left of the first tunnel. Rappel from the maple tree.

70. **Sufficiently Breathless** 5.10 A ★★
55' Pro to 1 1/2" Doubles at 3/4"
Superb route with excellent protection. Ascend via a minor crack and corner system just left of Winter Delight. Several fixed pitons. Exit right to the maple tree belay.

71. **Fall Guy** 5.10 D ★★
65' 5 QD's and optional pro to 3/4"
An exciting definitive face climb. Climb a shallow vertical corner to a sloping stance (loose rock just above) stepping up left and around corner to join with Aging Fags. Rappel from bolt belay.

72. **Aging Fags** 5.10 D ★
65' RP's, small wires and TCU's to 1"
A wide dihedral that is quite bold to lead. Starts off from a ledge 15 ft. left of the tunnel.

73. **Blownout Direct** 5.9
65' Pro to 1 1/2"
Climbs a free-standing thin flake, then pulls into a corner stance before ascending a piton protected seam. Rappel from bolts.

74. **Tombstone Territory** 5.7
25' Pro to 2 1/2"

75. **Bluebird** II 5.10 A ★
Multi-pitch Pro to 4"
One of the original Beacon favorites. An excellent 35 ft. crux pitch. The old starting point was located at a fir tree next to the base of Wild Turkeys. From there it traversed rightward via brushy, sloping ledges and minor downsteps. Otherwise climb one of a number of routes near the first tunnel to approach.

76. **Variation** 5.9
40' Pro to 3"
Halfway up the crux pitch of Bluebird, step left onto a good ledge and finish up a deep dihedral choked with bushes.

77. **Bridge of the Gods** 5.12 B or 5.11 A2
110' Pro to 4"
High above the first tunnel is an impressive shallow corner system that eventually widens to an offwidth crack splitting an arete. Two rope rappel. Approach via one of the lower variations.

78. **Pirates** (a.k.a. Rock Pirates) 5.12 A (R)
110' Pro to 2" Runout
Probably one of the three most awkward climbs at Beacon Rock. A very long lead with many fixed pitons. Still worthy of top-roping. Approach via one of the lower variations. Two rope rappel.

79. **Blownout** II 5.10 A ★★★
Multi-pitch Pro to 2 1/2" Doubles recommended

One of the ten supreme classics. Commence up Blownout Direct (or another nearby option) to a bolt belay. Move up left, then straight up a jagged hand crack to a belay in a protected corner beneath the great upper dihedral. Step forth and climb the obvious corner 120 ft. (crux) until possible to exit right onto a gravelly ledge.

80. **Second Wind** 5.11 D ★
100' Pro to 2"
Twenty feet up the last pitch of Blownout (1/4 bolt), traverse right around the arete and finish up a strenuous thin finger crack.

81. **Borderline** II 5.11 B ★★★
80' QD's and pro to 1 1/2"
A staggering and most excellent climb. Begin at the lone fir tree immediately right of the Wild Turkeys start. Climb up right onto a detached flake and climb (pitons) 40 ft. up (5.10+) to a belay on the "Beacon Towers" ledge. Step right and embark up the beautiful second pitch (bolts) via face climbing and laybacks to the top.

82. **Grunge Book** III 5.10 A A3
Virtually all of this route (except 40 ft.) has been free climbed.

83. **Excalibur** 5.12 B ★★★
80' QD's, small wires, TCU's (and Friends to 2 1/2")
Incredible! An extreme line and one of the most difficult at Beacon. Start on the "Beacon Towers" immediately right of Wild Turkeys. Face climb straight up until it eases and widens gradually near the top.

84. **Crankenstein** 5.11 A (TR)
35'
Immediately behind the lone fir tree at the start for Borderline is a minor dihedral corner.

85. **Wild Turkeys** III 5.10 C A2
Multipitch Pitons and pro to 1 1/2"
One of the original Beacon aid routes. The popular first pitch goes free at 5.10 C, but the second has still yet to be freed. Probable 5.12+. Ascend an interesting corner left of a fir tree. Climb 25 ft. to a belay on a sloping ledge. Continue up right via easy steps to the "Beacon Towers". Belay then nail the seam left of Excalibur.

86. _____ 5.12 (?)
120' (TR)
From the first belay on Wild Turkeys commence directly up a shallow dihedral. It soon straightens to a vertical seam on a perfect smooth face.

87. **Psychic Wound** 5.10 B
80' Pro to 1 1/2"
This climb and the following several routes are located above the second tunnel. From a stance at a thin oak tree step up right and climb a left facing corner (piton) to a stance. Finish up a weaving corner system until possible to exit left to the Flying Dutchman bolt belay.

88. **Flying Dutchman** 5.10 B ★★
80' Pro to 1 1/2" Small wires and TCU's suggested ⹁
An enjoyable route. Excellent rock. Begin at the thin oak tree and climb
up past two pitons to a stance. Continue straight up a left facing dihedral
to the bolt anchor. The upper pitches of the previous two climbs have yet
to be freed.

89. **Bears in Heat** II 5.11 B ★★
80' first pitch Pro to 2 1/2" Cams suggested
A great climb. The name describes accurately the second pitch bear hug.
Start as for Flying Dutchman past the pitons to a stance. Step left, then
ascend an unusual crack system to a crux move just shy of the anchor.
Rappel or continue up (35 ft.) the second pitch bear hugging and jamming
to reach a final belay. Rappel.

90. **Dirty Double Overhang** III 5.7 A3
Multipitch Pitons and pro to 1 1/2"
A long, multi-pitch aid route immediately right of the great roofs in the
center of the wall. The two pitches above Grassy Ledges offer good free
climbing.

91. **Smooth Dancer** III 5.9 A2
Multipitch Pitons and
pro to 2"
This is the other
sustained two-pitch
aid route on the
central face.

92. _____

93. **Takes Fist** III 5.10 D
★
Multi-pitch Pro to 3"
This wild climb leads
through a fist crack in
the 'great roof' area.
A little brushy on the
first pitch. Start near
the twin oak trees
angling up right to a
vegetated dihedral.
Commence upward
and through the
overhang to the top.
Rappel via another
established safer rappel
on Grassy Ledges.

94. _____

Robert McGown on Free For Some (5.10C)

95. **Ground Zero** III 5.11D ★

Multi-pitch   Small wires, TCU's and double sizes recommended to 2 1/2"
Seldom climbed in its entirety but one of the more challenging and
unusually physical leads. Each pitch is more extreme than the previous
culminating with a crux at the roof. Start near the twin oak trees up easy
5.9 slabs to a piton belay 80 ft. Continue up to a small lip (5.10 C) and
some difficult climbing to a bolt anchor on the left 80 ft. Another 25 ft.
lead to an anchor underneath the roof. Smear left (crux) around the
corner, then finish up a very steep crack to the top 50 ft.

96. **Nuke-U-Later** 5.10 C (R)

120' Pro to 1 1/2"
Start as for Ground Zero but a thin crack that leads up through flaky,
hollow rock. Anchor just below a small overhang. Rappel.

97. **Iron Maiden** III 5.11 A4

KB, LA, Baby Angles and Pro to 3/4"
Step left from the Nuke-U-Later belay and nail up a seam on a blank face.

98. **Flying Swallow** III 5.10 D (R) ★★★

Multipitch Pro to 3" Extra set of thin to medium wires
One of the better Beacon Rock classics. The present route starts up the
5.6 section of Dod's Jam then traverses rightward across to the top of
Black Maria, Reasonable Richard and Local Access. But it is much more
direct and fun to climb one of these three options mentioned above.
From that bolt anchor traverse up right to the base of a 60 ft. dihedral.
Belay, then have at it. This lead is unusually strenuous and involves
difficult protection placements. Stem upward (crux) to a sloping ledge and
bolt anchor. Above is a slightly overhung finger crack that opens to an
offwidth. Climb this to another ledge and belay. Then continue up a nice
left-facing corner 20 ft. to Grassy Ledges. Belay. Rappel via an established
descent route or finish up a flared chimney system to join with Dod's Jam.

99. **Variation** 5.10 B ★

60' Pro to 2 1/2" Extra wires

100.   **Direct Start** (to Flying Swallow) 5.11 A

100' (TR)

The following three climbs are good direct start options to Flying Swallow,
Flight Time and Blood, Sweat and Smears.

101.   **Local Access Only** 5.10 A

110' Pro to 1"
Wanders up easy but unprotected slabs to a small corner dihedral.

102.   **Reasonable Richard** 5.9 ★★

110' Pro to 1 1/2" TCU's recommended
Commence up easy slabs to a stance, then embark up a minor crack (1
bolt) on a rounded face leading to a bolt anchor. An excellent climb.

103. **Black Maria** 5.9+
110' Small wires, TCU's and Friends to 3"
A minor corner directly below True Grunt and just left of Reasonable Richard. Start up easy slabs but work left from a stance into a dihedral. Continue up this until you can exit right to the anchor.

104. **Flight Time** II 5.11 C ★★
Multi-pitch Pro to 1 1/2"
For the climber with strong wings here is a terrific and well-protected route. Move up right (from the belay at Reasonable Richard) along dirty ledges to a mostly fixed crack. This is the wild one. Desperately climb up using the right crack when necessary to a sloping ledge and belay. Step back left and continue up a stiff dihedral to a hanging belay. Rappel or continue up and exit out right under a roof to join with Flying Swallow.

105. _____

106. **Flying Circus** III 5.10 C (R)
Multi-pitch Pro to 4" Extra set of wires
Above Reasonable Richard is a crack (with a small bush growing from it) that opens up to an offwidth. A long lead. 165 ft. rope required. Joins Dod's Jam route in the great amphitheatre.

107. **Blood, Sweat, and Smears** II 5.10 C ★★★
165' Pro to 3" Double set of wires
A most excellent route and one of Beacon Rock's finest. Traverse up left from Reasonable Richard belay. Enter and climb the dihedral passing through several small overhangs and thin sections. Belay on Big Ledge.

108. **True Grunt** II 5.11 A
165' Pro to 2" Extra wires
A difficult and technical crux. Unique but seldom ascended. A very long lead.

109. **Steppenwolf** IV 5.11+ A0 (5.10 C to Big Ledge) ★★★
165' first pitch Pro to 2" Extra wires
This superb route is one of the best prizes at Beacon Rock. Start up the 5.6 section to Dod's Jam until possible to angle right to a bolt belay under a roof. Step up right around the roof and climb a long exhilarating dihedral. Pull through a final overhung jam crack to Big Ledge. Belay. Above are two beautiful cracks than join halfway up and then angle to the right. The right crack is Steppenwolf, while the left is a continuation of Journey to the East. Free climb up the right crack (5.11+) 60 ft. to a bolt anchor. Above are several more pitches of mixed free and aid climbing up the "Norseman's Head" to the west side hikers trail.

110. **Dod's Jam** III 5.10 C ★★★
Multi-pitch Pro to 3"

One of the all time Beacon classics. Very popular. Start up easy slabs (from the 3rd tunnel) leftward along a series of corners and small ledges. When you reach the base of the main dihedral (Free For All joins here) step up to the birds nest belay. Climb a crack that quickly becomes an offwidth (5.9) to a ledge aptly called "The Perch". Climb up past a tree via a crux (5.10 C) jam crack. Belay at Big Ledge. Rappel or climb the next pitches. Step right around corner and move up a series of wide cracks and offwidth chimneys (5.7 - 5.9) then angle up right along slabs to a sling belay. The far left side of the amphitheatre offers a crack - chimney system called Osprey Variation (5.9) while the right side has a short curving crack in a bulge which leads to numerous ledges and short 5.8 sections that lead to the West Side Trail. Origional route descended to Grassy Ledges.

111. **Dod's Deviation** 5.9 (variation) ★
45' Pro to 3"

112. **Journey to the East** IV 5.11 A4 Pins, Rurps and Hooks to 3 1/2"

113. **Devil's Backbone** 5.12 A ★★
80' Pro to 1 1/2"
Probably the finest example at Beacon of a crack that splits an arete. Approximately 20 ft. above the first belay on Dod's Jam move left via underclings to an arete. Climb straight up to Big Ledge. An incredible climb!

114. **The Norseman** 5.12 B ★★
60' 5 QD's and minor pro to 1 1/2"
This is the bolted route on the buttress of the 'Norseman's Head.' From Big Ledge climb up Steppenwolf until possible to move right to a rounded buttress. Ascend this to a bolt anchor. Excellent climb.

115. **Dastardly Crack** 5.9 ★★
165' Pro to 2"
Directly above Dod's Jam from Big Ledge is a large dihedral. Climb the corner, angle left and up easy steps to a bushy corner that leads to the west side hikers' trail.

116. **Squeeze Box** 5.10 B ★
165' Pro to 2"
An interesting fist crack through a roof. From Big Ledge angle down left until possible to turn a corner. Climb a dihedral and overhangs to rejoin with Dastardly Crack.

117. **Edge of Fear** IV 5.11 A4
100' Pro to 1 1/2"

118. **Free For All** 5.8 ★★★
150' Pro to 2"
Excellent route. A must for everyone! Just left of a large oak tree (left of the 3rd tunnel) is a detached free standing 25 ft. pillar. The left side is the Direct Start (5.10 A), while the right side is 5.8. Climb either.

From the top of the pillar continue up the obvious crooked hand crack until it joins with Dod's Jam at the first belay.

119. **Free For Some** 5.11 A ★★★
140' Pro to 2" TCU's recommended
A remarkable and demanding lead with excellent protection. Immediately left of Free For All is a thin seam. Climb this to a bolt anchor at 65 ft. then ascend the second half (5.10 C) or rappel.

120. **Windsurfer** 5.10 B ★★★
120' Pro to 3" Double set of wires
A popular and exciting climb. To find this good route look for a left-facing dihedral with three small roofs. Begin up a wide crack that ends at a ledge and bolt belay.

121. **Fresh Squeeze** (a.k.a. Squeeze Box Direct) II 5.11 D ★
120' first pitch Pro to 2" Pitons? (140 ft. second pitch)
On a face between Pipeline and Windsurfer are two crack systems. The right is Fresh Squeeze. Ascend the first pitch (5.11 C) to a ledge and belay. The second pitch steps up above the anchor, moves right and climbs a vertical face broken by a seam. Eventually enters a dihedral and eases (5.10) until it joins with Squeeze Box.

122. _____

123. **Pipeline** 5.11 B ★★★
60' Pro to 1 1/2"
Superb classic. A must for everyone. On the right side of the Arena of Terror is a thin, difficult finger crack that ends at a bolt anchor next to several overhangs. Ascend this and enjoy!

124. **Pipedream** 5.12 A ★
160' 1st pitch Pro to 1 1/2"
Little is known about the quality of this route, but it looks incredible! The route has been free climbed in very bold style (ground-up and red-point). From the belay ledge for Fresh Squeeze (1st pitch) step left and ascend a remarkable crack on a smooth face to an anchor at the base of an easy dihedral. Rappel with 2 ropes or continue up and join with Dastardly Crack.

125. **Pipeline Headwall** III 5.11 B
Multi-pitch Pro to 2"

126. **Silver Crow** IV 5.10 D A3
KB, LA, Rurps and pro to 4"

127. **Axe of Karma** IV 5.10 C A3
Multi-pitch KB, LA and pro to 4"

The following six climbs are located left of the Arena of Terror. The leftmost is the easy (5.7) approach arete to Jensen's Ridge and the other west side routes.

128. **Red Ice** 5.10 D ★
145' Pro to 2 1/2"
Just left of the Arena of Terror. Ascend easy ground to a loose, hollow section. Move up left and finish up a beautiful finger to hand crack in a dihedral. Bolt Anchor. Rappel with 2 ropes or ascend one of the upper climbs on the west face.

129. **Doubting Thomas** 5.10 C
145' Pro to 1 1/2"

130. **Boys of Summer** 5.10 B
145' Pro to 2"

131. **Fingers of a Fisherman** 5.10 B
145' Pitons and pro to 2"

132. **Crack of Dawn** 5.9
145' Pro to 2"

133. **Jensen's Ridge** III 5.11 A ★
Multi-pitch Pro to 4" including TCU's and big pro for OW
The physical crux is a thin tips crack on the second pitch, while the offwidth just beyond is certainly the psychological mindbender. Commence up an easy ridge (loose) to a bolt belay. Step right (nearly off the platform) and ascend the desperate thin crack 20 ft. to a ledge. Enter into a deep dihedral that opens to a wide offwidth. Belay at bolts just where Lay Lady Lay joins. Continue to the hikers' trail via two options. Both are 5.9+.

134. **Updraft to Heaven** III 5.10 D A1 (R)
160' KB and pro to 6"

135. **Mostly Air** 5.10 B
160' Pro to 2 1/2" (poorly protected)

136. **Lay Lady Lay** II 5.10B ★★★
100' Pro to 2 1/2"
A quality route except for the poison oak that plagues the start of this and the following three routes.

137. **Synchronicity** II 5.8 A2
Multi-pitch KB, LA and pro to 4"

138. **Rip City** II 5.10 A ★★
80' Pro to 1 3/4"

139. **Hard Times** II 5.10 C
80' Pro to 2 1/2"

140. **Rag Time** II 5.10 C
80' Pro to 2 1/2"

141. **Boulder Problem in the Sky** II 5.10 D ★★
Multi-pitch Pro to 2 1/2"
An excellent stem problem with a captivating roof crack exit move.

142. **Iron Cross** (a.k.a. On the Move) II 5.11 B ★
Multi-pitch   Pro to 4"

143. **Variation** 5.9
80'   Pro to 2 1/2"

Climbers on Horsetail Falls, Columbia Gorge Ice.

Columbia River Gorge Ice

The Columbia River Gorge is a favorite Pacific Northwest jewel, a photogenic wonderland that attracts numerous ice climbers with each winter freeze. Yet Gorge ice climbing, with its subzero temperatures and spine chilling winds challenges even the best climber.

Historically, ventures were made into this vast arena of ice during the 1970's to conquer some of the obvious classics. Their names ring in our ears, and like the cold winter wind their conquests stand true. Jay Carroll, Mark Cartier, Ken Currens, Alan Kearney, Monty Mayko, Jim Mayers, Robert McGown, Mike O'Brien, Jim Olson, Ed Newville, Jeff Thomas, Scott Woolums, Ian Wade and others. Famous ice routes like Crown Jewel, Shepperds Dell, Gathering Storm, and Shady Creek are several of the great classics ascended during that period.

Years later, during another mega-freeze, and with high-tech ice-climbing hardware in hand a new generation of climbers approached the ice. The result is a realm of modern Gorge ice climbing that has not been the same since. Bold test pieces like Life Shavings, Post Nasal Drip, Brave New World, and Dodson opened the eyes of climbers to a new and unlimited arena of ice climbing potential.

The Gorge offers a wide spectrum of possibilities from enjoyable wet plastic ice to vertical ice pillars or thin smears to multi-pitch desperate grade IV and V climbs still awaiting an ascent. The area of greatest interest to ice climbers in the Gorge starts near Crown Point, ends near Bonneville Dam including Cape Horn on the Washington side of the river. The concentration of ice routes is due to the easy access along the scenic highway which runs parallel with I-84 through this portion of the Gorge.

During the off season locals-in-residence usually suffice by visiting Eliot Glacier to hone skills. The glacier offers good and accessible crevasse or serac climbing. For the hard core enthusiast seeking the edge of adventure, visit the glacier from mid-September thru October. Superb ice conditions can be found throughout the Eliot and Coe Glacier region, while extreme mixed rock and black ice conditions are available higher up on the Eliot Glacier Headwall.

Other recommended options are the innumerable ice climbs found on the upper slopes of Mt. Hood such as Steel Cliff, Devil's Kitchen, Black Spider, and Illumination Rock during the winter months. At Pete's Pile during the same Gorge cold spell several excellent, steep and gnarly desperate ice climbs develop if you are looking for a hyper blast. At Government Camp Ski Bowl to the west of the main ski run is a prominent yet small, north facing basalt crag which offers thin ice climbing with just a 40 minute approach.

Search and you will find.

Climate and Access Information

Ice climbing in the Gorge is without a doubt moody, and when compared with rock climbing it might even seem a bit trivial. But when the northern arctic air mass descends upon the Pacific Northwest ice climbers scramble to sharpen their tools and race to the Gorge.

The sub-freezing temperatures tend to arrive between December and February. In roughly 3 days and with a steady surge of cold wind the ice routes are ready to be climbed, typically lasting only one to two weeks before melting, yet occassionally staying frozen for months.

A rather stiff, penetrating 15-40 mph east wind blows much of the time. Many of the routes though, are protected in corners or enveloped in forests which help break the main blast of the growling wind.

Water ice varies considerably from day to day, as well as from one climb to the next. On one route you may experience brittle "dinnerplate" ice or see 5 ft. fracture marks race across the ice as your tool strikes the surface. On another route you may find wet plastic ice that even a brick would stick to.

Generally, the greater the amount of water in the falls the less likely it will be ascended. A small seepage on a wall creates a beautiful thin delicate smear, whereas big waterfalls are simply unclimbable in their entirety, but may offer leads to the right or the left of the main watercourse. Most moderate ice routes such as Benson Icefall or Crown Point drip liberally with water. On certain routes an extended cold spell may be needed to slow the flow of water. Look beyond the obvious routes, then you will see the many smaller seeps that often are quite solid and drip much less.

Ice Ratings

In **The Ice Experience** (1979) by Jeff Lowe, two systems are incorporated to achieve a rather comprehensive and useful Americanized grading standard. They are the Yosemite Decimal System (mentioned in the Introduction) and the Scottish grading for ice. Let's take a quick look at the grading in detail.

The **length or vertical relief** (whether 60' or 600') conveys to the climber a picture of general route difficulties.

The **overall difficulty** grading (I to VI) should indicate to the climber the approximate time necessary for such an ascent.

The **hardest rock or ice** move (or both) will prepare you for the technical problems encountered on the climb and will be shown as WI (water ice) 1-7.

If aid climbing is part of the route, a rating of such will be added as well. For example, the final name and rating could look as such:

Ice Man 600' IV+ WI 5 5.10 B A2

As a reminder, since ice is a constantly changing medium, no rating should ever be considered absolute, but used constructively as a reference tool only.

Equipment

Basically, any ice climbing gear will work, yet modern equipment, as well as good technique will help improve efficiency.

Bring at least two ropes, especially if you are considering several wet routes in one day. While climbing, properly manage your rope by keeping it from direct contact with water as long as possible. A water saturated climbing rope quickly becomes a stiff "steel cable" refusing to feed through even the largest belay device. Since one frozen rope is better than two, keep the second rope in your pack until you need to use it. Reverse curved ice tools are the best choice for climbing, while plastic boots and rigid crampons are pretty much standard fare.

Aluminum or titanium ice screws, a small selection of QD's, several loose carabiners, some extra webbing for slinging trees or bushes, and you're set. Pitons are helpful, especially on extreme routes or when you need a fixed belay at a rock wall. Though seldom used, a bolt kit could be handy if you desire a more permanent anchor. Another creative anchor are 12" lengths of conduit tubing.

Proficiency equals common sense, reliable equipment, and hours of out-on-the-ice experience.

Clothing

When climbing Gorge ice for the first time, the cold east winds will feel brutally bone chilling. Bring a proper amount of clothing to suit your comfort level. For your survival you should dress well, even bringing extra warm clothes just in case. There is a thin line between feeling the cold temperature and being seriously chilled.

Most ice climbers will climb one or two routes in a day, and be fully satisfied. But for the hardman who likes to grit his teeth at extreme climbs, an early start will allow you to climb 3, 4 or even 5 different 1-2 pitch ice routes in a day. The grade IV and V ice routes will generally need a full day for success, including a start before sunrise and sometimes finishing after dark. Be sure to guarantee your retreat options, and to let your friends know what you're up to. Quickly, let's go ice climbing, before it all melts and tumbles down!

1. **Tunnel Vision**
   120' I WI 3 FA Jan. 1993 Wayne Wallace, Tim Olson
   Park on the south side of I-84 approximately 1/4 mile east of Tunnel Point where the railroad tracks cut through an outcrop of rock along the freeway. Walk east along the tracks until you see the icefall on your right. Further left deep in the woods is **Wind Tunnel** WI 2.

2. **Crown Jewel** (a.k.a. Crown Point)
   300' III WI 3 FA Jan. 1979 Alan Kearney, Chuck Sink
   A super classic and very popular ice climb in the Columbia Gorge. This

Wayne Wallace leading Life Shavings, Columbia Gorge Ice

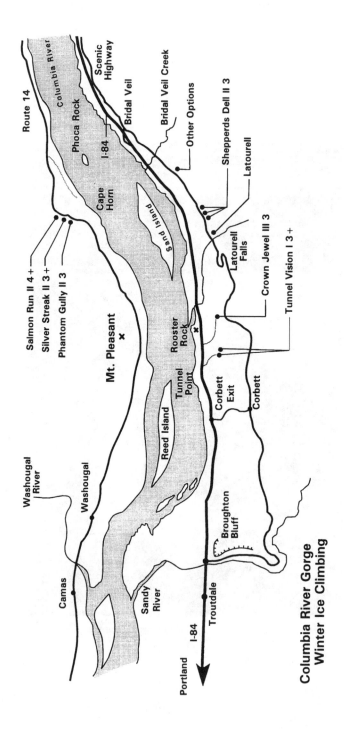

Columbia River Gorge
Winter Ice Climbing

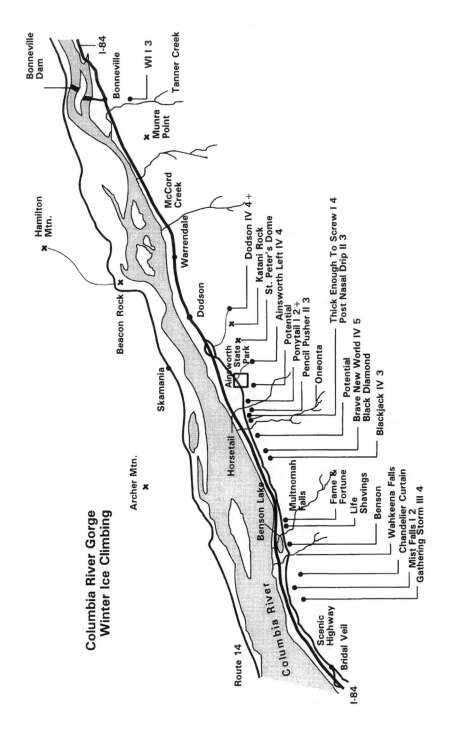

Columbia River Gorge
Winter Ice Climbing

Bonneville Dam

I-84

Bonneville

WI I 3

Tanner Creek

Munra Point

McCord Creek

Warrendale

Dodson IV 4 +

Katani Rock

St. Peter's Dome

Ainsworth Left IV 4

Dodson

Hamilton Mtn.

Potential

Ponytail I 2 +

Pencil Pusher II 3

Oneonta

Ainsworth State Park

Thick Enough To Screw I 4

Post Nasal Drip II 3

Brave New World IV 5

Black Diamond

Potential

Beacon Rock

Blackjack IV 3

Skamania

Horsetail

Archer Mtn.

Benson Lake

Multnomah Falls

Fame & Fortune

Life Shavings

Benson

Wahkeena Falls

Chandelier Curtain

Mist Falls I 2

Gathering Storm III 4

Route 14

Columbia River

Scenic Highway

Bridal Veil

I-84

moderately difficult icefall is quite obvious from the highway and holds a spectacular position for all to see. Because of the numerous parties ascending the route, it is wise to make an early start.

Park immediately across from the Rooster Rock pinnacle at a small pullout. Walk to the railroad tracks then east to the icefall (15 minutes). This 2 pitch climb is usually ascended on the left side where the least amount of water drips. Prepare to get soaked anyway unless the conditions are premium. The 2nd pitch eases to a large amphitheatre. Two options: Rappel or continue up the easy gully to the scenic highway and Vista Overlook. Then descend down an easy dirt gully west of the Vista House parking lot.

3. **Latourrell Falls**
   35' I WI 2
   Some minor, but limited, ice bouldering left of the main waterfall.

4. **Shepperds Dell area**
   This wind sheltered area offers several excellent options for leading. Drive west on the scenic highway (U.S. 30) from The Bridal Veil exit for approx. 2 miles. The climbs here are quite popular and will often remain climbable days after the other falls have collapsed. They are as follows from left to right.

A. **Original Route**
   60' I WI 2
   FA Jan. 1974 Phil Jones, Tim Carpenter
   A short ice climb leading to easy slopes above. Rappel from vine maples.

B. **Salamander**
   140' I WI 2+
   FA Feb. 1979 Jeff Thomas, Ed Newville
   Located approx. 100 yds. west of the Original Route.

C. **Water Heater**
   140' I WI 2+
   FA Jan. 1979 Jeff Thomas, Dave Jay
   Located approx. 50 yds. west of the Original Route.

D. _____
   150' I WI ?
   An often partially formed curtain of ice; usually a TR, but has been lead.

E. **Bent Screw**
   150' I WI 3
   FA Feb. 1979 Ed Newville, Jeff Thomas
   One of the first to form and last to fall apart because the water source is from seeps and not stream flow. Usually wet and muddy near top. Rappel from a convenient tree at the summit. Good climb.

F. **The Column**
   100' I WI ?
   FA Jan. 1979 Alan Kearney, Sheri Nelson

Short but steep climb with a larger volume of water. Needs an extended cold spell to freeze this climb. The ice formation around the corner is also available. Just a short strenuous lead.

5. **Bridal Suite**
150' I WI ?
FA Dec. 1985 Jeff and Bill Thomas
A good one pitch climb nestled in a bowl high above the road and below the trail leading to Angel's Rest. Long approach but other potential does exist nearby.

6. **Slippery Dolphin**
160' I WI ?
FA Dec. 1983 Mark Cartier, Monty Mayko
A steep and sustained lead located at the same pullout as the Gathering Storm.

7. **Pumphouse Blues**
Several quality routes located near the brick shed west of Slippery Dolphin. The 'Blues' route is a blast at WI 2+ while to the right are two half-tier ice smears called **Terminal Dysfunction**.

8. **Gathering Storm**
400' III WI 4 FA Feb. 1979 Jeff Thomas, Alan Kearney
Approximately 1 3/4 miles east of the tiny community of Bridal Veil (U.S. 30) you will find the staggering Thomas-Kearney route. Park at a dirt pullout near a steep 160' bluff of rock. The waterfall immediately south of the road is the Slippery Dolphin. Hike the upper plateau south uphill to the next large cliff. Ascend the obvious major frozen waterfall. A short, steep first pitch leads to a huge bowl. The last is the longest and hardest.

9. **Mist Falls**
200' I WI 2
A relatively easy single pitch climb directly beneath the wind-whipped falls. Either climb up into the alcove and rappel or exit right to rappel from the trees. Expect a crackly suit of armor! Park at a large signpost just before Wahkeena Falls and hike directly up the stream bed to the cliff.

10. **The Chandelier Curtain**
An impressive 300' massive curtain of hanging ice curtain worth visiting. Does connect but not likely climbable.

11. **Smooth Operator / (Sweetest Taboo)**
100' I WI 3
FRA Dec. 1990 Wayne Wallace, Tim Olson (W.W., Lane Brown)
Park at Wahkeena Falls and take the right side trail. After a zig zag scramble directly uphill a distance towards two ice gullies. The right one has not seen an ascent (100') while the left is Smooth Operator. Both climbs fade into dirt and rock gullies. Rappel from nearby trees, or continue up the gully to a hidden ice lead called **Sweetest Taboo**.

12. **Wahkeena Falls**

Good for photographing, but too many tourists.

13. **Benson Lake Icefall**
165' I WI 2-3
Quite possibly the most frequently climbed chunk of ice in the Gorge.
Often has 3-4 groups attacking the wall at the same time. Located approximately 1/2 mile west of Multnomah Falls and immediately across from
Benson Lake. Expect liberal amounts of dripping water. Nonetheless, it is
here that most climbers stop and check into the sport. There are easy
slabs on the right and left with numerous trees for belays. Topping out
can be quite technical depending on the thickness of the ice.

14. **Dressed To Chill**
160' II WI 3+ FA 1993 Tim and Cindy Olson
Approximately 150' left of Benson Icefall proper are two vertical smears
that ease back at 30'. Dressed to Chill is the right and longer variation that
continues up on ice steps ending with a vertical, hollow chandelier that
fades to dirt slopes at the top.

15. **Variation I**
100' I WI 2

16. **The Classic**
100' I WI 2
Further left is an excellent low angle problem. Starts wide and becomes
narrow higher up. Liberally protected with trees and bushes for anchors.
The last section is usually too wet to bother with, but the lower half is
very popular.

17. **Pleasure Cruise**
40' I WI 2+
Deep in the trees 150' left of Area Classic you can find a fun, quality route
that ascends past a small tree and abruptly ends on dirt slopes above.

18. **Ice Cooler**
40' I WI 3
Located around corner from Pleasure Cruise.

19. **Shady Creek**
200' II WI 3
FA 1979 Ken Currens and Monty Mayko
Located up and right behind the lodge at Multnomah Falls. Although the
area is crowded with tourists the climb is quite secluded. Involves two
short leads of steep ice with one near vertical ice bulge to finish. Rappel
from nearby trees.

20. **Multnomah Falls**
Always terrific to see, especially when the falls are encased in ghostly
curtains of ice. In Jan. 1979 Jeff Thomas and Ed Newville climbed the
right side approximately 200' and called it "The Once and Future King".
At present the main amphitheatre has F.S. restrictions against access.

21. Life Shavings
80' I WI 4
Stellar route of the highest standard. Located just east of Multnomah Creek in a tight corner.

22. Fame and Fortune
200' II WI 3
Premium quality climb and readily accessible. Top out to the woods above, then hike down to the east. The crux is the first and last sections. Best if done in two short pitches. Located east of Multnomah Creek.

23. Blackjack
500'+ IV WI 3
FA Dec. 1990 Wayne Wallace, Tim Olson
Located at mile post 21 on U.S. 30. A very exciting and challenging route with many pitches of moderate climbing. Park to the east of m.p. 21 at a large pullout, then hike up west on Gorge trail #400 and directly up to the base of a detached pillar (will be connected only after a mega-freeze). To begin the 'moss variation' walk right 100' until you can angle up to a mossy arete on the right side of another gully system. Bushes for pro and belays. Angle up left til you can rappel into the main drainage. Ascend 3 main ice tiers, the last being a little wet near the top.

24. Brave New World
500' IV WI 5
FA February 1996 Wayne Wallace, Tim Olson
A bold venture of the extreme kind that set a new standard for the Gorge. This stellar classic is located immediately left of the Black Diamond. Formed by wind spraying the stream flow left onto the vertical wall, creating a fragile and technically extreme chandelier crux section half way up the ice route.

25. Black Diamond
500' approx. IV potential
Located 1/4 mile east of mile post 21 at the dirt pullout next to a small bridge. Brave New World is the left route and this is the right one in the large west facing amphitheatre. The route offers outstanding exposure from start to finish and is vertical for over half its distance with ice umbrellas before easing back to 60°+. The first 20 ft. of the main icefall seldom forms. The first 50 ft. has seen an attempt.

26. _____
200' approx. Potential
A colorful climb with many tiers above the first slope. Has yet to see an ascent beyond the first 80' pitch. Park to the west of Oneonta Gorge at the trailhead. Hike up westward to the base (20 min.) of this ice climb. The first pitch is gently angled 65° ice to a bush belay, followed by a vertical ice pillar ending in forested slope on the second pitch.

27. Oneonta Gorge

A good photographic stop with yielding no ice climbing interest.

28. Post Nasal Drip
200' II WI 3

A terrific, enjoyable route. Located east of Oneonta Gorge 1/2 mile at a small dirt pullout. Easily visible just uphill through the trees. The right and larger icefall is 20' wide, and is separated into two vertical sections. Both are sustained, while the second pitch fades near the top. Possible to exit left after the first pitch and rappel from trees (95 ft.).

29. Thick Enough to Screw
95' I WI 4

FA Dec. 1990 Tim Olson

To the left of the previous ice climb is a fabulous vertical ice smear. A classic testpiece.

30. Horsetail Falls (a.k.a. ...And The Horse You Rode In On)
200' III WI 5 FA Jan. 1993 Bill Price and Tim Olson

Here is proof that any ice can be climbed. A modern testpiece of phenomenal proportion, ascending the right side via the angels wings. A route that breaks with tradition and climbs on sacred ground.

31. Pencil Pusher
200' II WI 3

FA Dec. 1990 Wayne Wallace, Tim Olson

Uphill and to the right of Horsetail Falls are several exciting ice problems. Pencil Pusher is the central ice smear with a pillar at the second vertical step. The first pitch is a beautiful 70° ice smear. Finish up the right side of the pillar. An excellent option and not at all very difficult. Other potential lines exist to the left as well. To rappel, move right and down to near the edge of the cliff to a tree with a rappel sling. Perfect 80' rappel.

32. Peter Piper
90' I WI 2+

FA Dec. 1990 Tim Olson, Jay Green

To the right of Pencil Pusher is a short, fun ice climb. An easy lead on mostly slabby ice. Fades into the brushy hillside near top. Angle left to the rappel tree.

33. Ponytail
80' I WI 2+

A good, 70° ice climb that sees numerous ascents, particularly the first 80'. Located approx. 150' left of Horsetail Falls and offers easy access. Oh, yes, there is a second pitch (WI 4) on the upper right with no pro.

34. Ainsworth Left
700'+ IV WI 4 (to high point)

This is THE ultimate Columbia River Gorge classic ice route. Yes, it has been seriously attempted numerous times by very strong parties of climbers. All were impressed. To succeed an extended day will be necessary from dawn to dusk. Drive to the Ainsworth State Park overnight camp area and hike south via a trail and creek drainage to the Ainsworth Creek amphitheatre. On the left face is this stellar super classic. Very wet ice near top of route.

35. **Dodson**
700'+ IV WI 4+ (to high point) Feb. 1993 Bill Price, Tim Olson
South of the tiny community of Dodson and east of Katnai Rock is the huge vertical face of Yeon Mountain. The route is located near the left arete and can be seen from I-84. All of it has been climbed except for the large hanging chandelier of ice on the last pitch.

36. **Tanner Creek Ice**
50' I WI 2
At the Bonneville Dam exit, turn south onto a graveled road that soon ends. Just beyond you will find several good easy to moderately angled ice climbs protected from the wind. Fun climbs.

37. **Starvation Creek**
200' II WI 3 FRA Dec. 1985 Scott Woolums, Terry Yates
Park at the Starvation Creek trailhead (eastbound I-84). The icefall is climbable and there are several other possibilities nearby as well. A little exploration is all that is needed.

The following ice climbs are situated along the Washington State side of the Columbia River. To gain access to these drive east from Camas-Washougal on State Route 14.

38. **Cape Horn Area**
Easily one of the most impressive sights to see from across the river, these ice routes will readily capture the imagination. Of the nearly limitless possibilities, many are desperate WI 3 ice leads (or harder) and often 200'+ in length. There are three tiers. The lowest tier is available by hiking along the railroad tracks westward 15 minutes from an access road to the east. Little is known of the ascents here, but most have been climbed. The central tier ice routes seldom invite. The upper tier lies above the highway and just east of the steel chain-link protection nets. Cape Horn are highly technical, unrelenting and long.

The known routes for the upper tier are as follows:
A. **Hanging Curtain**
80' I WI 3+
FA Winter 1979 Ian Wade and Scott Woolums

B. **Dodge City**
80' I WI 3
TR Winter 1979 Scott Woolums, Ian Wade

C. **The Pillar**
80' I WI 3+

FA 1979 Ian Wade, Scott Woolums

D. **Phantom Gully**
300' II WI 3
FA 1979 Monty Mayko, Robert McGown

E. **Silver Streak**
300' II WI 3+
FA 1979 Monty Mayko, Robert McGown

F. **Salmon Run**
300' II WI 4
FA Dec. 1980 Jim Olson, Robert McGown

Bill Price leading Salmon Run on Columbia Gorge Ice
122

Adventure Climbing

For those of you born of the *wild breed*, this supplemental rock climbers digest will hopefully encourage you to seek exciting new alternative places for your climbing repertoire.

This section is designed to entice you to explore beyond the urbanized confines of Portland. These one day adventure climbing options are readily accessible, and are within a few hours drive from Portland. All are unique! Several are in the Columbia River Gorge, while other places are at higher altitudes along the Mt. Hood scenic corridor, or south toward Salem.

For example, Horsethief Butte offers many short bouldering and top-rope problems, while other places like Illumination Rock or Razorblade Pinnacle are summits of unusual stature. The crags to the east of the Cascade range have more sunny, dry days than the cliffs in Western Oregon, while the high altitude crags are especially suitable for climbing when the summer temperatures soar into the 80's.

Take the initiative, and make your climbing passion go beyond the vertical numbered 5.*whatever* horizon and explore this realm. After all, you are not just an average individual, and the following pages are anything but *normal*.

Rooster Rock and Crown Point Area

One of the most popular pinnacles in the Columbia River Gorge would have to be Rooster Rock. The standard **South Face** route is an enjoyable climb and is roughly 160 ft. high, offering interesting 5.4 rock climbing. The east face route is 5.6 (R) and starts up next to a leaning tree, then embarks up left on steep ground to join with the regular route. The other routes on Rooster Rock are serious leads and are seldom ascended.

Crown Point is the 500' north facing scarp immediately south of Rooster Rock. The historic and panoramic Vista House is situated upon its summit. There are five known routes on the prominent north face. Expect difficult climbing on vegetated and occasionally notorious loose rock.

The **Zucchini Route** (NE Face, 5.6 A2 or 5.10) aims for a big slice of an offwidth pie, high and just left of the summit. The **Ripping RURP** 5.10 C (X) A2+ branches up right from the zucchini ledge. High near the top of the cliff, is a bolted 5.12 route called **Jewel in the Crown**.

On the far right side a dark gash seperates the main massif from a cigar-shaped dome of rock called **Alpenjager**. The deeply sliced corner system is called **West Chimney** (5.4). Left of West Chimney is a prominent, but little known crack system climb splitting the right face of the main wall.

Another good option is the Pillars of Hercules which are located approximately 3 miles east of Rooster Rock, just west of Bridal Veil. The Pillars are a group of basaltic towers and cliffs ranging in height from 60 ft. to 120 ft. high. Of the five known routes available on the main Pillar the standard **East Side** route (5.4) begins on the southeast side of the pillar. Ascend up 10 ft. under a prominant notch and climb the left hand corner system. From where the climbing eases traverse onto the north face to the base of another chimney, then continue to the top. Two ropes are needed for the rappel. The minor **Pinochle Pinnacle** (5.4) is located on the cliff face further east. Although these interesting clusters of pinnacles are readily available most are infrequently ascended due to location and a substantial layer of moss growth.

Chimney Rocks

An isolated, inspiring cluster of pinnacles scattered along a sub-ridge extending down from Silver Star Mountain. If the crag were situated in Portland it would surely be a very popular climbing area. The outcrop is well situated on the ridge with breathtaking views of nearby mountains and the Columbia Gorge.

The crag is composed of andesite-mantled diorite and is generally good quality rock. A fair number of crack routes are available, as well as some interesting face climbing. At present, rock climbs vary from 5.6 to 5.11.

Approach by way of State Route 14 to Washougal. Take State Route 149 for 6.5 miles to County Road 11. Follow this road 3.9 miles to the Larch Mountain Road. Portions of the final 2 mile road along the ridge are heavily rutted and brushy. Rather than 4-wheeling up the road park the vehicle and hike in.

Cigar Rock - Cape Horn

Cigar Rock is located near the east entrance of the BNSF railroad tracks tunnel exits from Cape Horn. The several pillars here are notoriously difficult to ascend due to the nature of the rock—notoriously loose, and that is an under statement. Yet for those hardy individuals here are the logistics.

East Couloir II A2, or x-rated free 5.(?) rating. From the beach, climb a narrow chimney between the main wall and the pinnacle. Scramble up the debris gully to the saddle seperating Cigar Rock from the main massif. Climb up a short corner to an airy stance then ascend (aid) totally rotten rock 30 ft. to top. Yes, more than a few people have backed down off this one. **North Face Direct** II A2 for 50 ft. to summit.

Immediately west of the tunnel is the **Tyrolean Spire** II A1 5.(?) a 230 ft. pinnacle that is approached by walking the escarpment above. Rappel 100 ft. into the chimney between the parent cliff and the spire. Swing out onto its north face and climb directly to the summit using direct aid as needed.

About 600 yards off shore from Cape Horn in the midst of the great Columbia River is the small island called **Phoca Rock**. A visit here is especially fun when combined in a day of canoeing or kayaking along the Washington or Oregon shore. A small gravel cove beneath the north face offers the only feasible landing spot. One navigation hazard exists in the way of a reef which extends northward from the east side of the cove for about 100 feet at or below waterline. A wide berth should be given on approach due to strong currents. The most likely point of departure is Dalton Point boat ramp 1 1/2 miles west of Multnomah Falls. The ascent of Phoca is a scenic scramble.

Little Cougar Rock

Cougar Rocks (Winema Pinnacles) protrude from the south wall of the Gorge between Multnomah and Oneonta Creeks at approximately the 2600' level. For the infamous I-84 rock climbing hound this is a probably must.

Three optional approaches are available: Park at Multnomah Falls and ascend the Larch Mountain trail, then branch over to the Trails Club lodge. Or park 3/4 mile east of Multnomah Falls, and ascend the Elevator Shaft trail which zig zags up a long talus field, then bushwack to the main trail, then just west of the Trails Club lodge follow a descending trail toward Big Cougar. Descend east of the ridge, skirting the base of Big Cougar till you can access the saddle between BC and LC. These two approaches are time consuming but scenic.

A third option is a two hour grunt via the stream drainage immediately east of the pinnacle. Ascend the stream gully till a small vertical waterfall forces you to the right. Ascend the dirt and talus slopes near the creek and aim for the upper saddle of Little Cougar.

On Little Cougar expect about 200' of technically easy but occasionally loose 5th class rock climbing. The summit is a short, delicate balance move. There are several other seldom climbed routes on the pinnacle (west and east ridge) that are quite extreme and bold.

St. Peter's Dome

Southeast from Ainsworth State Park is a historical and prominent feature of the Columbia Gorge. The dome was quite popular up till the 1960's but now relatively few climbers set their sights on this serious endeavour. An ascent of the main Dome by *any* route is extreme and terribly loose.

The **South Face** route (III 5.6 A2) contours west from the saddle 80' then up to Furrer's Cave, then up the 96 ft. band of rock to the next ledge before jogging left past a tree. Ascend a 52 ft. band of loose rock to a slope of very loose moss covered scree that leads to the top. The **Saddle Direct** route (III 5.6 A3) ascends directly from the main saddle to the 96 ft. band.

The **Northeast Face** (III 5.6 A3) traverses along grassy ledges to a rock shoulder, then continues traversing to a point directly below the north face cave. Ascend to the cave then left and up 90 ft., then right 50+ ft. then continue up 80 ft. on steep rock and moss, and then some. For specifics research older books such as the Neuberger or the Dodge guide.

Or, consider combining a hike up Rock of Ages trail and a descent of the

Mystery Trail (involves two rappels). Then, ascend the **Little St. Peter's** as a *finalé*. This 60 ft. pinnacle of rock yields a commanding view of the Dome and surrounding area, while offering a less hazardous experience. Rappel anchor in place. Pro? Well—there is a piton halfway up!

Immediately east of St. Peter's Dome is **Katanai Rock** on the northwest edge of Yeon Mountain. A cross country bushwack but still a unique adventure in itself. Expect some roped climbing.

Rabbit Ears

Deep in the heart of the scenic Columbia River Gorge, and north of Bridge of the Gods is a unique hike leading to the summit of Table Mountain. Low along the southern exposure of this mountain are the Rabbit Ears. The Indian name is Ka'nax and To'iha. An afternoon sun will sometimes rivet these two small ears against an ethereal blue sky.

Least you might think this to be a casual tour hold onto your camel. For those who wish to proceed do so with the enthusiasm of a hunt, because the Rabbit Ears are indeed a remarkable summit for the adventurer. The quality may be less than desirable so don't expect great rock, but rather a challenging climb with a captivating view.

Approach the rock by hiking a portion of the Table Mountain trail which leads past Aldrich Butte, then bushwack east through secluded forests of young alder trees across the old landslide. The final slope leading to the technical part of the climb is quite steep.

On a narrow spit of soil seperating two cataclysmic gullies (one of them you just came up), begin the climb. Eighty-five feet of 4th class scrambling brings you to an anchor, then aim right around a corner, and up toward (5.4) the notch between the ears. There are several adequate belay anchors, but since the natural protection is skimpy a piton or two is recommended.

Windy Slab

Located along State Route 14 at the base of the south side of Wind Mountain. Windy Slab is a low angle 40' slab with half a dozen TR. The rock is reminiscent to granite friction climbing and routes range from 5.4 to 5.10 C. Park in a gravel pullout *west* of the "Keep Skamania County Clean" sign. Windy Slab is highly worth the casual passing through visit.

Horsethief Butte

A very popular, traditional place for teaching beginners as well as escaping from the mid winter blues. The crag offers limited lead routes and is best suited for bouldering and top-roping. The longest climbs are situated on the outside of this fortress-like crag. Before the 20th century local Indians frequented the area, and today the place is under the protective jurisdiction of the State Parks of Washington. When the weather is showery in Portland, you can often find reasonable sunny though windy conditions at the Butte. The crag is roughly 30' high on the inner walls. Beware of ticks and poison oak.

Take I-84 east to exit 87 just east of The Dalles. Cross the bridge over the Columbia River and drive about 3 miles north to State Route 14. Turn right (east) and drive 2 1/2 miles passing Horsethief Lake State Park. Park near a state park sanctuary sign just beyond a small bridge. Walk south and enter via one of several hidden entrances leading to the inner corridors.

Dog's Tooth

On the south flank of the famous Dog Mountain is a sharp profiled backbone arete of rotten rock and moss rising for 2000 ft. from the the river edge. Worthy? Absolutely—in fact for those who are looking for an alpine-like challenge, scrambling up to Dog's Tooth and climbing the short 5th class summit, then continuing up the highly exposed ravines near the backbone arete to the summit trail of Dog Mountain is a superb adventure in itself and a Gorge classic.

Pete's Pile

Provocative Pete, the hand that tweaked,
The man that turned to stone.
A dream so sweet, he could'nt beat,
Grinding knuckles to the bone.

Pete has worked very hard to create an exciting wonderland of rock for the local climber on a prominent basalt cliff overlooking the East Fork Hood River near the Cooper Spur road. The place is finally earning a long overdue respect thanks to diligent efforts from local Hood River climbers. The rim-rock is quite extensive and steep, 200 ft. in height and perhaps 1000 ft. in length. The rock has much to offer in terms of nearly limitless future route development, yet only about 35 climbs have been established so far, from 5.6 to 5.11. There are some climbing restrictions on certain sections of the wall.

Drive south from Hood River on the East Fork Hood River Highway (35) for a total of 23.3 miles. Park at a dirt pullout on east side of the highway (the pullout is 3/4 mile south of the Cooper Spur Road and 1/3 mile north of the East Fork Trail #650).

An easy 5 minute approach trail angles leftward uphill toward the crag from the pullout. Pete's Pile is an excellent multi-season climbing area generally free of snow from April through October.

French's Dome

This unique and highly accessible dome of rock lies amongst a tall canopy of evergreen trees along the lower west side of Mt. Hood. There are at least a dozen climbing routes available ranging from 5.6 to 5.12. Most are fixed with bolts, practically eliminating the need for natural protection. The overall

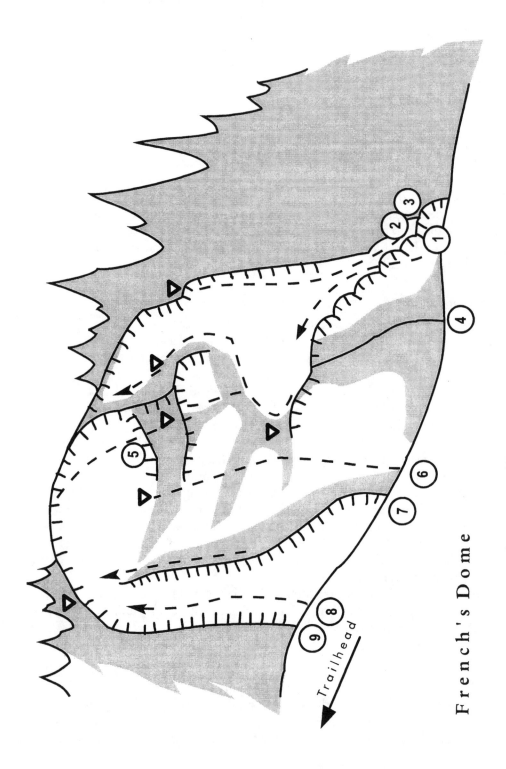

French's Dome

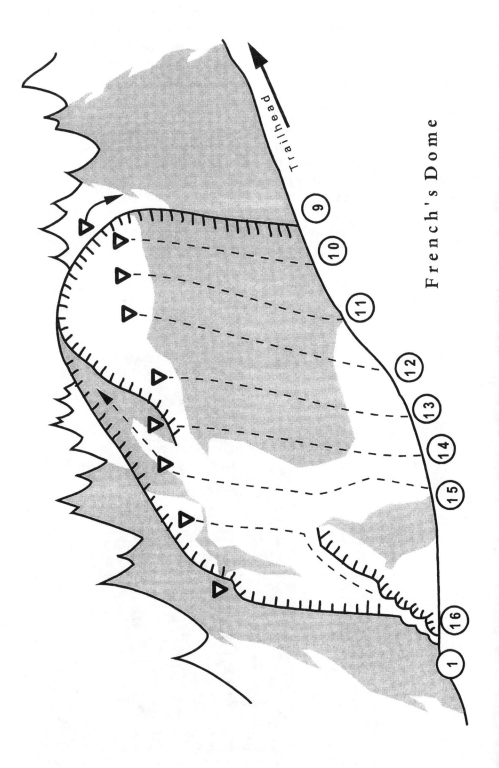

French's Dome

height is 160 ft. from the longest side and 80 ft. on the road face.

The crag is located 6.2 miles up the Lolo Pass Road (F.S. 18) from its junction with U.S. 26 at Zig Zag. Look for an unobtrusive dirt pullout on the right. The dome is *not* visible above the forests of Douglas Fir trees. Take the trail (1 minute) to the crag and explore this interesting geological wonder of the Oregon woods. French's Dome is a peaceful climbing area situated far from the hustle and bustle of real world politics. Misty Slab is the visible sloping buttress of rock located 40 minutes uphill from French's, yet because of the brushy approach ascents there have been kept to a minimum. At the present rate of erosion at the cliff base of French's Dome, the whole rock may soon roll downhill, but quickly followed by an enthusiastic herd of rock climbers with quickdraws in hand!

The routes at French's Dome are described clockwise, beginning with the ever popular Giant's Staircase. The older climbs tend to be a little runout, but still entertaining.

1. **Giant's Staircase** 5.6 ★★★
   QD's and runout
2. **Tin Tangle** 5.8 ★★★
   QD's and runout
3. **Do it Again** 5.9 ★
   Left of Tin Tangle on same blocky rib.
4. **Variation** start at **Giant's Staircase** 5.6
   No pro
5. **Static Cling** 5.10 B
   QD's
6. _____ 5.11-
   QD's
7. **Yellow Brick Road** 5.10 B
   Pro to 3" and runout
8. _____ 5.12+ ?
   QD's
9. **Road Face** 5.12 A
   QD's
10. **China Man** 5.11 B ★★
    QD's
11. _____ 5.12+ ★
12. **Pump-O-Rama** 5.12 A/B ★★

Climber on crux pitch, Razorblade Pinnacle 5.10 B

13. **Crankenstein** 5.11 C ★★★
14. **Silver Streak** 5.10 B ★★★
15. **Straw Man** 5.8 ★★
    QD's and runout
16. **Alpha Centauri** 5.8 ★★★
    QD's and good pro to 1"

Razorblade Pinnacle

This superb, isolated mountain jewel is a true alpine experience located at the 5800 ft. level just below the Sandy Glacier. Seperated by two deep river chasms, the profile of the "Blade" captivates all who tread near, giving the climber a postcard perfect view of the stark west face of Mt. Hood. Approach by way of the Lolo Pass road (F.S. 18). Take F.S. 1828 near the McNiel-Riley campgrounds. The road winds uphill to a gravel side road leading to the Top Spur trailhead.

Hike the Top Spur trail, and then follow the Bald Mountain (Round the Mountain) trail south into the vast Sandy River basin. Take the southernmost drainage of the Muddy North Fork Sandy River. Follow the stream upward until the foreboding canyon walls steepen. Angle leftward up the steep hillside to the SW base of the Razorblade Pinnacle.

The **Gillette Arete**, 5.10 B (or 5.9 AO), ascends the western most corner, and is an excellent multi-pitch alpine climb. Pro to 2" including cams. Start by scrambling up a leftward leaning ramp on the south face to a fir tree, then step around tree to the main notch that overlooks the northside chasm. Embark straight up the prow for two short leads or one long lead. **Leadhead and Pieplates** 5.7 A3 is the left corner of the same arete and begins by a traverse in from the regular route at the notch. The **Indirect East Arete** is an exposed meandering 5.8, and the **East Arete Direct** is also 5.8. The ultra classic route **Desert of Reason** IV 5.4 A4 is a serious yet exhilerating aid line that ascends the smooth overhung north face of the 'Blade.'

The south face rappel route is called **Machete**, and goes free at 5.9 and offers good protection. Start by scrambling up the same ramp to the fir tree belay. Then step up right on steep ground (fixed pins) which quickly eases to a slab. Then angle up right, smear across the crux and up right to the next belay just above a small cedar tree. Follow close to the remainder of the rappel route upward to the summit.

To descend from the summit, rappel via an easy tree to tree descent on the south face of the crag (can be done with a single 165' rope). One long day is usually needed to hike the trail (3 hour approach hike) and ascend the pinnacle.

Salmon River Slab

Drive south from Zig Zag on F.S. 2618 for approximately 3.8 miles. At a pullout next to a good fishing hole on the Salmon River you will find a 75°

angled black slab 60 ft. high and about 70 ft. wide. There are several free routes available. They are as follows.

1. _____5.7   6 QD's
2. _____5.9+   9 QD's
3. _____5.7   8 QD's
4. _____5.9   5 QD's
5. _____5.3   8 QD's

Ski Bowl and Multorpor Slab

Located south of U.S. 26 at Government Camp. Multorpor Mountain is the hill on the left, which offers several low angle slabs, while on the right is Mirror Mountain. Park and hike up the ski area to the obvious rocky outcrops. Government Camp climbers-in-residence have explored these crags, and other nearby outcrops such as near Trillium Lake. During the summer months the Multorpor Ski area is host to mountain biking races, and an alpine slide.

Illumination Rock

This challenging sharp profiled alpine peak is situated at the 9500 ft. level on the SW slopes of Mt. Hood. The peak offers exposed, and less than perfect rock. The approach generally takes 2-3 hours from Timberline Lodge. Climbing routes range from 5.6 to 5.11, but do beware of the hazards such as loose rock (wear a rock helmet). Face it, this is bold climbing. For those who are mysteriously drawn to Illumination Rock, you are certain to find many challenges and rewards. Most of the original routes were pioneered by Gary Leech, Bill Blanchard, and Ray Conway.

1. **West Arete** II 5.3
   Ascends up past west gable, then surmounts a steep step and follows ridge to summit.

2. **East Arete** II 5.5
   From the saddle ascend past the grand tower and elevator shaft to top.

3. **North Wall** II 5.5
   Traverse from the saddle west above Reid Glacier. Meander up till you can crawl through the skylight.

4. **South Face** II 5.4
   Ascends the inner face of the main south chamber.

5. **South Ridge** II 5.7
   Ascends the ridge on the right of the south chamber.

6. **South Chamber** II 5.4
   Climb the inner left side of the chamber via corners that eventually lead to west gable.

During Oregon's long winter months, when Mt. Hood is covered in a mantle of snow, Illumination Rock offers the totally honed alpine climber numerous exhilerating rime ice ridges and ice gullies to ascend. Without doubt Illumination Rock, Steel Cliff, Eliot Glacier Headwall, and the Black Spider will put a spark in the wildest dreams of any alpine climber. **Castle Crag's Direct** is now an established summer rock route for those who are interested in high altitude precarious climbing. Climbed in 1994, the route proved surprisingly easy (III 5.7). One must wonder why in the blazes no one had crossed this wild ground before. But, the climbing is said to be good for the 5th class sections, and rotten for the 3rd and 4th class sections.

Newton Pinnacle

This surprising and secluded rock pinnacle, is perched high along a forested ridge above the Hood River Meadows parking lot. Park at the gate and walk to the ski run, then angle rightward and hike directly toward the main pinnacle (or take trail #667). A minor thrash uphill through the woods brings you to the west face. A 45 minute hike. The west face is approx. 80 ft. high, 165 ft. long, slightly overhung, but with a liberal amount of hand holds.

1. **Wage Slave** 5.10+ ★★★
2. **Poison Pill** 5.10C ★
3. **Logisticon** 5.11A ★★★
4. **Neophytes** 5.9 ★★★
5. _____ 5.10+ ★★
6. _____ 5.10
7. _____ 5.11

Lamberson Butte

This extensive climbing area stands like a castle wall overlooking the magestic alpine slopes of the wooded Newton Creek drainage. Sheer rock cliffs, green forests of mountain hemlock, glacial moraines ablaze in red heather, and a view of the fearsome Black Spider combine to make Lamberson a remarkable destination for the veteran climber.

The wall averages 150'-200' tall, and is grouped in three main sections. These are subdivided further into large buttresses of rock reminiscent to granite walls. At present, the climbs range from 5.8 to 5.12.

By far the most visible, and perhaps the most staggering is **The Great Pig Iron Dihedral** (5.12 A, or 5.10 A2+). Like ocean waves, this 160' undulating dihedral glimmers in the sunlight, even from afar. Another super classic is **Bag of Tricks** (5.10 C), which ascends up ledges, thin corners, and face climbing next to a large slice of rock.

There are routes of every make and color: smooth-as-glass dihedrals, lightning bolt cracks, aretes, flake cracks, high-angle face routes and even several roof problems.

Pig Iron Wall

Loose

Approach

Ground-up climbing frequently becomes the method of ascent at Lamberson. Thin pitons, and bolts are usually necessary for success. Ground-up leading is bold, but also rewarding for those who like a fine mixture of free and nailing options. Beware of loose rock, especially when you are exploratory climbing.

Park at the Hood River Meadows trailhead and hike toward Elk Meadows on trail #645. Take trail #646 following Newton Creek uphill to the Round-the-Mountain trail #600. An excellent shortcut can be made by hiking along the creek through light brush for the last 1/2 mile of the approach. Ford the stream and angle up toward one of the crags. The southwest facing wall lies partway uphill overlooking the Newton Creek drainage. The hike is an easy 1 1/2 hr. 3 mile approach.

Pig Iron Wall

1. **TR** 5.10+ 120'

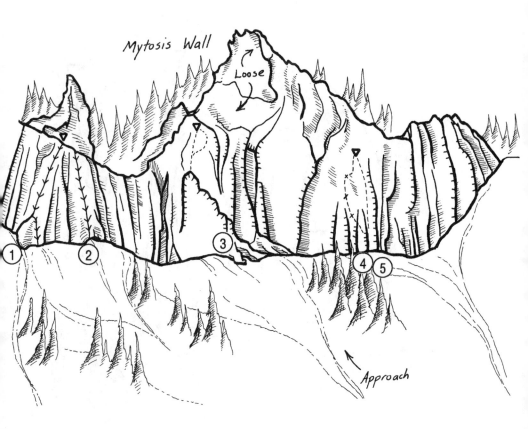

2. **Pig Newton** 5.10 D ★★
   120' Pro to 2"

3. **The Great Pig Iron Dihedral** 5.12 A (left seam 5.10 A2) ★★★
   150' Many KB, LA, TCU's and pro to 1"

4. **Headhunters** 5.11 B ★★★
   150' TCU's, RP's and pro to 1 1/2"

5. _____

6. **Panorama** 5.8
   165' Pro to 3"

Mytosis Wall

1. **Trafficosis** 5.8
   150' Pro to 2"

2. _____

3. **Mytosis** 5.10 C ★
   Multi-pitch Pro to 2" Cams recommended

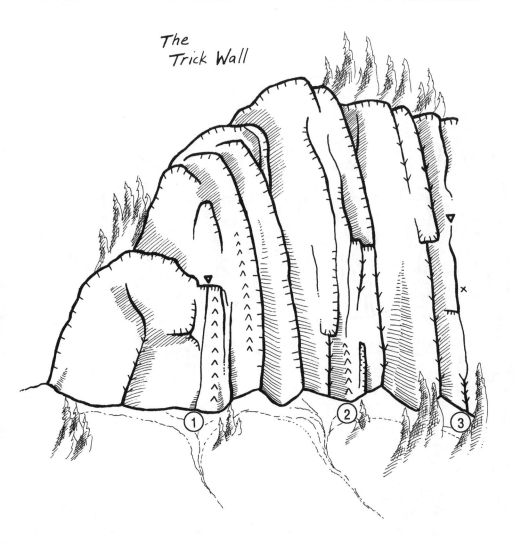

The
Trick Wall

4. **Thirty-six Light Years** 5.11B or 5.9 A2 ★★★
   155' Pro to 2" TCU's suggested
5. **Catch Me If I Fall** 5.11 ★
   165' Pro to 2 1/2" Needs fixed gear

Trick Wall

1. **Poultry Picnic** 5.9
   60' Pro to 3"

2. **Pencil Arete**
   60' TR

3. **Crash of the Titans** 5.10 C ★★★
   100' Pro to 2 1/2" Cams recommended

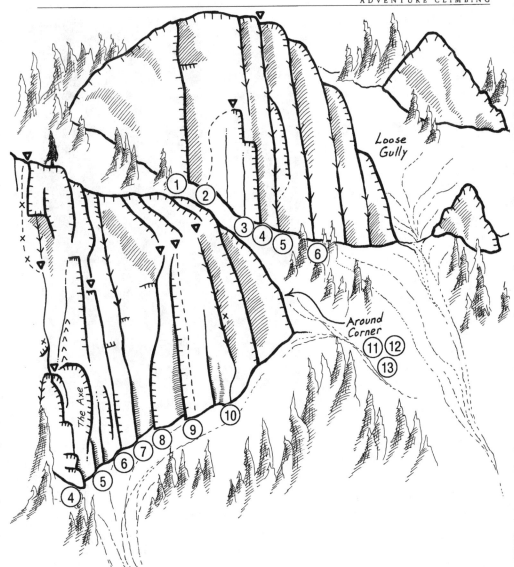

4. **Bag of Tricks** 5.10 C ★★★
   Multi-pitch   TCU's, RP's and pro to 3"

5. **Variation Start** 5.10 A
   60'   Pro to 1 1/2" including pitons

6. _____ 5.12 (?)
   80'   TR

7. _____

8. **Trafalgar** 5.10 C ★
   80'   TCU's, Friends to 3" required

9. _____ 5.11B
   80'   QD's ★★

137

10. **The Test Tube** 5.10 A A0 (R)
    80' Pitons and pro to 2"
11. **Quantum Gravity** 5.8 ★★
    60' Pro to 3"
12. **Pushover** 5.10 C ★★
    60' Minor pro to 2"
13. **Sunset Bowl** 5.9
    80' Pro to 3"

Upper Trick Wall

1. _____
2. **Papa Tule** 5.10 A1
   80' Pitons and pro to 2"
3. **Lightning Bolt Crack** 5.12+ TR
4. **Mama Jamma** 5.10 C ★★★
   80' Pro to 3" plus cams
5. **The World is Collapsing** 5.10 C ★
   150' Pro to 3" plus cams
6. **Sacrosanctimonium** 5.10 B ★★★
   165' Pro to 3" including cams

Climber leading Mama Jamma (5.10C)

Bulo Point and The Pastures

Bulo is located roughly 10 air miles east of Mt. Hood. These unique odd bumps of rock are nestled among the tall Ponderosa Pine forests on a dry, and generally sunny, eastern facing slope. Bulo Point has for a number of years been the abode of hunters, hikers, and mountain bikers, and even the occasional rock climber.

At Bulo Point an inviting, well established footpath quickly escorts you from the old dirt road to the crag. This is the original climbing crag in this part of the country. A generous selection of quality leads or TR's are available as well as superb views of the arid desert of north-central Oregon. On a lower road to the east you can explore the classic climbs at the Boy Scout Crag, or walk in the Pastures where an endless array of TR and bouldering opportunities exist. Most of the boulders in the Pastures are 50' or less in height and fit the description of *little bumps* in the woods. Bring extra long webbing to set up TR or just boulder practice instead. Moderate routes (5.6 to 5.10) abound, but cracks tend to bottom out. And when the horizontal flakes angle the right direction tantalizing roof climbs are created. Zeeks in paradise!

Drive south from Hood River, OR on U.S. 35, or drive east from Sandy, OR, past Government Camp and over Bennett Pass. National Forest road 44 begins between Sherwood campground, and Robin Hood campground. Follow road 44 about 10 miles to road 4420 (leads to Bulo Point), then drive south approximately 1 1/2 miles. Take a narrow dirt road to the left (#240) for roughly one mile and park where a distinct footpath leads through the trees to the top of the outcrop.

The **Pastures** and the **Boy Scout Crag** are located further east on F.S. 44. Take a sharp right turn (SW) onto road 4450. At about 1 mile the Dufur watershed sign will be visible at an intersection. The paved road straight ahead leads to Hairpin Rock on road 4450; a right turn leads to the Pastures (road 4421), while another immediate right from 4421 onto the closed road 4421-621 ends immediately at a dirt mound and leads to the Boy Scout Crag. Quick access to BSC is available by walking 5 minutes from the dirt mound in a north westerly direction into a small creek drainage.

East of Lookout Mountain on trail #458 about 1 mile and on the south facing slope that drops into Badger Creek Wilderness is the **Heliotrope Pinnacle** (5.7), an 80 ft. high pillar of rock. The area is quite beautiful and can be combined as a dayhike in the area by starting at High Prarie or at trail #456A which starts at Fifteen Mile campground just south of Bulo Point. There are other unique possible objectives along the Lookout Mtn-Flag Point trail so bring the binoculars and enjoy the vista.

Callowash River Crag

The Clackamas River seems like one of the last places you would go to climb, right? But, even here, along the Callowash River you can find challenging roadside climbs. Do beware when visiting these crags. Stay on the few established routes; for loose rock awaits just out of sight. The steep, mossy slopes above the road can be dangerous to the unwary.

Just left of the main section of wall is a smooth near vertical 80 ft. cliff which offers one 5.10+ route, and two 5.11+ routes (TR only). The classic here has got to be the **Johnson-Watt** route (5.9), which ascends 130 ft. of rock on the main wall and is practically all QD's.

Drive SE of Estacada along the Clackamas River on Hwy 224 to Ripplebrook, then south on F.S. road 46. Take the Callowash River road. Look for an extensive roadcut several miles up river. Near the upper left end of the roadcut you will find most of the climbs. Do not get hit by a blind motorists racing madly up to Bagby Hot Springs. After the climb, and if the weather is hot, you can step across the road to swim or fish, and still be on belay—almost!

Stein's Pillar

Stein's Pillar is still a highly sought after prize worthy of climbing. Both of the origional routes can be free climbed. To reach the Pillar, follow U.S. 26 east from Prineville, then when nearing the east end of Ochoco Reservoir turn north on Mill Creek Road. Drive approximately 5 miles and turn right onto F.S. road 500 that leads to the trailhead. The trail is about 1/2 mile long.

The **Northeast Face** III 5.11A offers exhilerating climbing on very steep rock. Stem the chimney just above a cave on the northeast side and belay on a large ledge. From the right side of the ledge climb a corner, then face climb up and left to a second ledge. Step left, then continue up to a bulge. Move up left, then back right and climb an overhang to a large ledge halfway up the face. Move to upper ledge, then power up and left past an overhang and continue up left to a large black knob. The last pitch leads straight up the overhung wall to the top. Two rope rappel.

The other original climb is the **Southwest Face** III 5.10D. Ascends an obvious dihedral system, then traverses left and face climbs straight up to an overhang. Work left under the overhang to its end. Power over the buldge and traverse back right, then climb the crux buldge above. Continue up a left slanting crack and face climbing to the top. Rappel the north side route.

Harlen Roadside Quarry

Would a little bit of steep, quarried basalt out in heep country seem inviting? It may be worth the visit. All the routes here are totally bolted considering the nature of the rock (somewhat loose and dirty). The wall extends for roughly 250 ft. and is 40 ft. high on the left and 120 ft. on the right. The crag is quite steep at nearly 80°, with a total of seven free routes as of 1993. The routes range in difficulty from 5.6 to 5.11.

Drive south to Corvallis, then west on U.S. 20 to the small community of Burnt Woods. Turn south on the paved road for 10 miles to the tiny cluster of houses called Harlen. Turn right (west) onto a gravel road for several miles, passing an overnight camping area. Approximately 1/2 mile beyond is the crag on the right.

The Menagerie

Here is a fascinating and protected wilderness area situated along the wooded south facing slopes of the South Santiam River near the community of Upper Soda. The rock pinnacles near Rooster Rock are quite solid and fun to climb, while the shapes of all the pinnacles are contorted and unique. Yet the favorites here are plentiful. The great **Turkey Monster** is absolutely staggering and has probably seen a bare handful of ascents since Eugene Dodd, Dave Jensen and Bill Pratt completed it in 1966. The most frequented crags are Rabbit Ears, The Arch, Turkey Monster, Panorama Point, Rooster Rock, and Hen Rock. There are a newer selection of bolt routes on several of the pinnacles such as at Rooster Rock, but you might inquire about the seasonal access closure (bird nesting habitat) *before* driving to the Menegerie.

Wolf Rock

This remarkable 900 ft. monolith of basalt casts a dark and forboding appearance down upon all who draw near. Even the easiest route is a long and tenuous 3rd class scramble. Yet Wolf Rock is an absolute 'must do' on everyone's list.

One of the most incredible Wolf Rock ascents took place here in 1972 when Wayne Arrington and Mike Seely ascended the south face headwall through the dark and awe-inspiring roofs. They called it **Barad-Dûr** (Dark Tower) IV 5.9 A3. This seemingly improbable route presently can be free climbed via a 5.11A variation at the roof. The rock offers numerous other routes. Nearly all of the climbs are done ground-up, so expect lengthy runouts.

Drive SE from Albany on U.S. 20 through Sweet Home until you approach Iron Mtn. Take F.S. road 15 south for approximately 10 miles to the Meadows. Turn west on the same road (F.S. 15) and park at one of several pullouts near the rock. A minor 15 minute approach brings you to the base of the wall. Be prepared for big-wall climbing if you intend to summit out. Wolf Rock can also be approached east of Eugene along the McKenzie River on F.S. road 15 at Blue River Reservoir, or F.S. road 2654 which is about 10 miles east of McKenzie Bridge.

Opal Creek Wall

Call it what you will, but Mr Bill, this wall is totally stellar. A miniature big wall, all 220' of it, and a real shocker to all who visit.

Climbers have ventured to this phenomenal crag on the Little North Santiam River east of Elkhorn; even as early as 1985. A friend once told of the secret place to another friend who remarked, "Seen it, been there, done it!" But few can boast a statement like that. And why should you hold back when a mega-classic route like **Steel and Stone** is waiting. This route is quite comparable to Wolf Rock's Barad Dûr. The climb can be ascended at 5.10B A2, or attempted at 5.13, twelve foot roof and all.

When visiting Opal Creek Wall and venturing beyond the few established routes you most likely need pitons, a bolt kit, and lots of stamina. This wall has the look and feel of granite which is certainly a surprise for any resident of Oregon. Huge sections of blank vertical rock, intersperced by overhangs, small and large, give Opal Creek Wall a unique high altitude appeal.

To make a selective analysis of Opal Creek Wall drive east from Salem on U.S. 22 to just east of Mehama, and take the Little North Fork Road into the Elkhorn valley. Continue up road #2207, then #2209 past Henline Mountain trail. Where the road turns left into the Stack Creek drainage, stop and feast on the unimaginable. Park near the culvert. Walk to the stream, cross to the other side, and where the two streams split, follow the rounded ridge spur directly up and away from both streams toward the cliff. A rough bushwack 45 minutes up the forested slopes brings you to the wall.

1. **Steel and Stone** II 5.10 B A2 (or 5.13 ?) ★★★
   220' KB's, LA's, and pro to 3"
   Opal Creek super stellar test piece of the finest standard. Ascends the wall
   left of the main buttress. Start up right about 40' from a large tree. Lead
   up odd ledges and steep 5.8 ground to a belay. Step right into a left facing
   corner then dance delicately left to 5.9 crux corner before ending up
   further left at a sloping ledge belay. Crank a 5.10 B section then smear up
   the infamous smooth slab under the great roof. Aid through the mega
   roof, and then up easier terrain to the top.

2. **Monty Piton** II 5.10C ★★★
   220' Pro to 3" including cams
   Starts at a lone thin fir tree left of the central buttress. Angle up left on
   steep, but reasonably easy 5.7 terrain to belay just below the Great Roof.
   Step up to and surmount this obstacle (5.10 C) and continue up the
   obvious dark stained left-facing corner to the summit. Highly exposed exit
   moves at the top. Rappel route.

3. **Belstein-England**
   220' Pro—most likely!
   Ascends one of the deep corners to the right of the central buttress.

Tumble Lake Area

Just north of Detroit lake at the headwaters of Tumble Creek you will
find a tantalizing group of pinnacles. The area offers superb opportunity for
photography with stark contrasting steep forested slopes, pinnacles and a
majestic view of Mt. Jefferson.

Drive east from Salem on U.S. 22 to a left turn onto F.S. 2223 just prior to
the town of Detroit, OR. Follow the French Creek road (2223) till it tops out
at Sardine Pass. The trail from Sardine Pass descends all the way to Detroit
Reservoir but a popular hike is to the rounded knoll of Dome Rock. Or take
the 800 ft. descent trail down to Tumble Lake for a bit of fishing and a good
healthy workout hiking back. On a ridge seperating Opal Creek from French
Creek is a minor pinnacle called **Dog Tooth Rock** that can be accessed by
hiking along the Marten Buttes trail that overlooks both valleys.

But, to approach the most elusive summit of all, start at Sardine Pass, hike
east past Dome Rock knoll to the classic 150 ft. spire called **Needle Rock**.
This spire has seen just a mere handful of ascents since Jim Nieland's second
ascent in 1968. Commence by scrambling up the initial section up to a single
fir tree belay. The route is generally nailed (A1) on the first pitch (but could
be free climbed at approximately 5.9) while the second pitch is free climbed at
about 5.8. Two rope rappel. Expect wide crack climbing gear and some loose
rock.

To explore the next fabulous area drive along the dirt road past Knudson
Saddle and park at a pullout in front of Watchtower Mountain. Hike cross
country up through slopes of bear grass and thick forests eastward till you are

above a narrow ridge that descends steeply toward **Tumble Rock, Split Spire** and **Elephant Rock**.

Tumble Rock is easy but exposed 4th class, Elephant Rock is easy, exposed 5th class with a lot of scrambling, while the infamous double summited Split Spire (5.6 A1 or 5.10) requires a fairly versatile rack of gear. Expect friable rock even on this classic summit. Two rope rappel recommended. The views on this portion of the adventure are spectacular.

And yes, it is true—the distinctive "elephant" shape seen on the skyline when driving west from Idahna is the upper summit—Tumble Rock!

Triangulation Peak - Boca Cave

Another classic area above Detroit is the Triangulation Peak area. Here you can pick handfulls of huckleberries in September while enroute to the crags. The views are impressive. Mt. Hood to the north, with Mt. Jefferson, 3Finger Jack, Mt. Washington and the Three Sisters yielding a panoramic view from this vantage point. The destination of course for most hikers is Boca Cave, but for the adventure climber there are several other challenges as well—**Spire Rock** an **X-Spire**.

Drive east of Detroit through Idahna and take F.S. road 2233 left to the McCoy Creek shelter. Continue east to the trailhead and hike 1.5 miles to Triangulation Peak. Spire Rock is the first major pinnacle that the trail zigzags past on the way to the overlook. Ascend the SE Corner on 5th class rock. Two rope rappel recommended. Then hike to Triangulation Peak, then follow a descent trail eastward in a thick forest till the trail cuts left underneath an outcrop of rock. Here you will find the unique east facing 30 ft. high Boca Cave. Bring a camera for the rewarding view of Mt. Jefferson taken from *inside* the cave. The elusive pinnacle on the east side of Olallie Butte is visible.

Immediately in front of the cave and slightly north is X-Spire, an interesting easy 5th class pinnacle. Single rope rappel is possible. The lower trail is immediately below this spire and can be used as an optional return loop hike.

Shark Rock Scenic Area

In Washington state near Randle, both **Kirk Rock** and **Shark Rock** offer an interesting alpine rock climbing adventure. The area is wooded but the trail follows along ridges with unique viewing sites along the way. From U.S. 12 at Randle, Washington head south on Hwy. 131 and in one mile head south on F.S. road 25. Continue south for 21 1/2 miles, then turn east on F.S. 28 for 2 1/2 miles which leads to Mosquito Meadows. turn right onto F.S. road 2816 and follow this for very rough road 4 1/2 miles to the trailhead. Take the Badger Ridge Tail #257 to the Boundary Trail and follow this east about 2 1/2 miles to Kirk Rock. Kirk Rock offers several pitches of alpine rock climbing. Shark Rock is a bit further along on the trail to the east.

Where F.S. road crosses the Cispus River you can see the nearly vertical 1900 ft. diorite tower called **Tower Rock**. The one known route on it is 5.8

and involves mixed free and aid climbing, but is certainly a worthy objective for the serious adventurer.

Adventure Thrashing

Canyoneering, orienteering, bushwacking, thrashing—whatever you desire to call it. You have heard about it. You have seen photos of it, and you have read about it in far away places like Utah and Arizona, but can it be done here in the great Pacific Northwest? Yes! This is the realm of Xavier Masters.

The activity of thrashing is an intense challenge with an unlimited realm. Adventure thrashing is a contrast opposite of crag climbing, and a an activity more comparable to the pioneer-explorer method of approach. There are no climbing ratings to fuss about, no politics, no rules, no high mountain summits, just a reason for survival against the elements. Total off trail, back woods adventure to the extreme.

Are others doing it? Read of Mark Dale and his quest for challenge in the Cascades and the Olympics where he describes everything from light scrambling to extreme brush beating in his analogous Cascade Bushwack Rating System.

Read of the *Alaska Mountain Wilderness Classic* where Roman Dial, Carl Tobin, George Ripley, Dick Griffeth and others find tremendous challenge traveling light, and fast across miles of trackless Alaskan tundra and mountain ranges.

Read in Christopher Van Tilburg's book *Canyoneering* where he details much about the sport elsewhere, yet includes several elusive photos of the Columbia River Gorge.

Or perhaps you have heard of Kurt Diemberger's quest for adventure in unusual places where few have ever been.

The possible starting points are really unlimited but here are a few generic clues. Mindolivich to Mystery Trail, NE Buttress Yeon Mtn., the Nesmith Patagonian Trade Route, Shooting Gallery on Indian Point, Wooly Horn ridge, Dog Creek, and much, much more.

Are the adventures technical? Occasionally a rope may be needed, but even more important is the ability to follow bear or deer trails, negotiate thick brush, climb over 5th class forest blowdown, orienteering in deep forest, ascend near vertical walls of moss, fern and vine maple, stream crossings, hornets nests, and more. Are the adventures serious? Always! Rewarding? Well—for those who have taken to the challenge, you might ask them, for they *never* look back.

The Hardman List

Broughton Bluff

1. **Gandalf's Grip** (complete) 5.9+
2. **Dynamic Resistance** 5.10 D
3. **Sheer Stress** (complete) 5.10 A
4. **Physical Graffiti** 5.10 D
5. **Dracula** 5.12 A
6. **Superstition** (complete) 5.11 A
7. **Lost Boys** 5.10 D

Rocky Butte

8. **Phylynx** 5.11 B

Carver Bridge Cliff

9. **Uncola** 5.11 C
10. **Smerk** (complete) 5.11 A

Beacon Rock

11. **Fear of Flying** 5.10 B
12. **Fire and Ice** 5.11 B
13. **Ten-A-Cee Stemming** 5.10 C
14. **Blownout** 5.10 A
15. **Borderline** (complete) 5.11 B
16. **Flying Swallow** (complete) 5.10 D
17. **Blood, Sweat, and Smears** 5.10 C
18. **Steppenwolf** (to Big Ledge) 5.10 C
19. **Free For Some** (complete) 5.11 A
20. **Pipeline** 5.11 B

Xavier Masters, eldest son of a wealthy Estancia landowner, lived much of his early years on the vast Pampas of Argentina. His heritage and his future were there on the plains east of the great mountains. Xavier was a man who gave his all, not only for the homeland but for the glory of the family crown, as well. He was a man of infinite detail, yet also a man of action, firmly founded in strength and resolution, a proud and mighty product of success which only a member of the Masters family could produce. His faithful family retainer Niguel, readily carried all the burden. Niguel continually served the Masters for many years, and was loyal even to a fault.

Xavier's father of course, was the Governor-generalé of a southern Pampas province near Olavarría, and as the son of an honorable first citizen Xavier was educated in the arts of the "bluebloods" from the finest schools on the European continent. For gentlemen of the Pampas, and particularly those of the Masters family, were expected to thoroughly learn the standards of honor and glory for the future of the family crown.

For years Xavier Masters had roamed freely across the highlands of Argentina climbing many terrifying Patagonian summits, even desperate spires like the Towers of Tyme and Payne, just to prove himself. Yet his father always said to him, "You will not receive your family honors from inside your own borders. You must go north, my son."

One day while Xavier and Niguel were crossing through El Presidenté's ecologically sensitive forest in search of the great X-Spire, a question of principle occurs. They stumbled upon a Schelaxia Oil Company survey team preparing to drill a test hole, prospecting for who-knows-what.

Soon, El Presidenté hears of Xavier's forest adventure, and concludes that he is getting too close to personal business. A chase ensues. Green uniformed mountain police comb the hills for Xavier and Niguel. They are forced to flee the country.

With nothing but his ever present manservant Niguel, and their proud mountain spaniel named Boomba, Xavier makes his escape north—just as his father once said. On horseback they traveled north along the very spine of both continents until they came to the Pacific Northwest, to an outpost called *El Arrgun*, a place that reminded Xavier and Niguel so much of their own homeland.

Having fled a police state, even here Xavier and Niguel feared the green uniformed mountain police. One day while climbing on a local cliff in their famous Patagonian style, they reached the summit only to find the much feared local mountain police—a cranky Scotsman—who infamously informs them, "Yerrr style n' peeetonz r' not vveelcomb heeerre!"

Thus, Mr. Notorious was born. And so Xavier *"alias Mr. Notorious"*, Niguel and their plucky spaniel Boomba daringly blaze across the Pacific

Northwest making bold new first ascents on virgin summits...mere steps ahead of the law. Like the wind and the clouds that blow through the Queen of Rivers Gorge, Xavier and Niguel conquer, then evaporate like a wisp of vapor. To this day they take their raw Patagonian style to the extreme, in search of truth and honor, always to the ultimate edge.

Upon summiting a tall peak during their adventures northward Xavier exclaims, "There 'tis!" pointing a long thin finger at a sharp rock spire on a peak far away. "That is what we've been looking for—as soon as we are there, then we *will* have honor, then we can surely return to the Pampas of Argentina, to our homeland, with "true" honor. Yes, both Xavier and Niguel desire to see their home province once again. For Xavier, the office of Governor-generalé awaits, and perhaps even El Presidenté's lovely unwed daughter. For Niguel, his dear, devoted wife and three small children beckon for a swift return.

Xavier Masters father, the Governor-generalé is getting on in years, and tyrannical forces are at work pressing against the borders of their homeland in Argentina. The Governor-generalé will eventually relinquish his office to one of his capable, honorable sons—*perhaps it will be Xavier!*—one who can effectively hold onto the office of political affairs. Someone forthright and strong will need to free the people from encroaching outside forces. And if the times do not improve soon on the vast plains of the Pampas of Argentina....

As Xavier and Niguel rode their horses northward they passed seven great shield volcanoes. Covered in winter snows these sentinels stand high along the crest of the mountain range effectively holding back all the forces of nature except one—the Queen of Rivers. Xavier, desiring to continue north to Ileskea found his destination blocked by this deep, swift river that cut through the heart of this forested mountain range. Upon seeing this river coursing its way from the vast hinterlands of the interior he wondered, "How could such a river have come to exist?" Xavier surmised, "This must be a place of great power."

Xavier and Niguel advanced to the north no further. Looking neither east nor west, Xavier instead turned and pointed his finger at the high isolated scarp to the south of the great river. Niguel looked at Xavier and nodded. For Niguel, an opinion was not necessary, it was not asked—he merely agreed with Xavier and both ventured forth.

These maverick *gauchos* of the Gorge, with heartfelt enthusiasm eagerly explored the ridges and stream beds of seldom traveled byways. Xavier, Niguel, and their mountain spaniel Boomba merrily toured secret castles of the gods. They crawled along steep precipices through narrow portals, past vertical rock towers into lush hidden valleys. Each hidden dell was a delight to explore. They were refreshed by the challenge, the dark clouds of gloom lifted. Here among the eternal forests, scrounging amidst vine maple, squeezing past prickly devils club, they sensed—the answer must be *here*.

One day, while delving along the inner sanctum of a remote stream drainage, captivated by cool, mist ladden waterfalls and moss covered cliffs,

Xavier Masters and Niguel met a stranger. Near the creek bed casually leaning against an old log sat a reclusive hermit. He was quietly minding his own thoughts, knife in hand, whittling on a project. Xavier thought to himself, "Am I hallucinating—is this all a dream?" The old hermits clothing, well-worn wool knickers and a leather pouch, were strangely dated, reminding Xavier of a wanderer from another time. A long cane, reminiscent of an alpen stock, lay by his side. He appeared to be more than just ordinary, and indeed he was; his name was Vern.

Xavier and Niguel had met an instant friend. Vern freely gave secrets of the Gorge in minute quips of detail. The Argentinian gauchos leaned close to Verns' many words becoming enveloped in a thick, silent mist of intrigue and tale. A blanket of thick pea soup fog wrapped close around them as the man of mystery babbled on. Finally, his words slowed down. The tone of his voice dropped ever so slightly, and he said, "—ave yoo zeen de boat?"

Xavier and Niguel lurched, their ears were instantly pricked. "*Hmmn?* Boat! What boat?" Their eyes riveted on Vern.

And so the forest hermit told them of the great carved ship deep in this very drainage in which they presently stood. Vern said to them, "—ah been 'eer feiteen 'ears in zearch of thiz great ship, an' Ahm steell lookin'—but it'z 'eer—ah knowa t'zz."

Xavier and Niguel bid Vern farewell and started to walk away, then turned to look back once more, but Vern was not there. It was as if he had never been there at all.

Months later, after Xavier, Niguel and their faithful Boomba had fruitlessly searched beautiful drainage after gorgeous creek bed in search of the great ship carving, they longed for another chance encounter with the elusive hermit—eager to ask him more questions, but they could not find him. All that Xavier and Niguel could see were the ravens circling overhead, and the ravens kept calling, "Vern! Vern!"

Xavier and Niguel charge forward with intense determination of will to find *"de boat"*. High above, an elusive summit lay easily within their grasp. They are here to conquer. Niguel Aleandro Pedro de Gonzales III, drenched with sweat and wielding a great long machete in hand, hacks away at the steep vegetated slope of hillside leading to the summit which Xavier is certain holds the great secret. *"Ahh!* The jungles of El Arrgun," declares Niguel, "they are as challenging as the jungles of my own homeland." Niguel soon passes the crux of the climb, and exhilarated at the thought of sure success he begins humming the Argentine national anthem—*Mmm, mm, na honra—mmm, mm, tierra natal.*

Xavier, belaying from a narrow ledge twenty meters below hears the distinctly familiar tune. Stimulated with pride for his homeland he breaks forth into a loud booming guttural gaucho version of the anthem. *Tierra de honra, Mi tierra natal, Argentino!* Xavier grabs a rack of pitons and beats the set loudly against the trunk of a tree in tune with the melody. The rhythmic sound of that glorious Argentine national anthem sweeps the hillside, echoing up and down each valley and dale. *Tierra natal, Oye! Argentino!*

Niguel, further aroused by the tempo and driven with national fervor, beats the machete blade against his climbing helmet in tune with the anthem. Cheerfully, the two wilderness gauchos thunder the hearty melody with robust Argentine intensity. Boomba, left behind to guard the packs, stands near a tree in the valley far below, howling mournfully. Perhaps he is excited by the national anthem as well, or perhaps he is little upset with all the racket and trundling of rocks that ricochet off the nearby cliffs.

Niguel, continuing upward toward the summit reaches for a hummock of moss, but it rips loose from the soil and he goes for the *big slide*. The climbing rope, racing through a carabiner and sling tied to a thin twig, momentarily comes taut. The bush peals free from the dirt hillside, and in a mass of tangled rope and flying debris Niguel tumbles downward landing abruptly on the ledge at the feet of Xavier Masters. Xavier analyzes him suspiciously and comments about his lack of caution, yet praises him for his national zeal. The gauchos of the Gorge shrug off the mishap, then set to piling small branches and dried leaves together for a campfire brew of *yerba mate*. Needless to say, neither gaucho made the summit—that day.

In their peculiarly *Xaviesque* sort of way they do what they want, when they want, and wherever they want. For although their style may seem like no style at all—it is quite original, and forever Patagonian.

Out on the Pampas of Argentina,
In a land where we were born there,
Where the prospects for finding the answer,
Were mighty thin,
So we went forth together,
To the north to find fair weather,
Seeking truth, and honor, and glory, just to win.

After months that stretched like an eternity in passing, they stumbled upon a vital clue. They discovered an elusive symbol etched upon a rock wall deep in a creek drainage. Here was the *"sign of the condor"*—just as a mysterious wanderer had told them long ago. Verns ravings became the catalyst in their search for the prize, and now his words brought renewed hope and vitality to their lives.

Xavier and Niguel had seen the markings years before—somewhere. Could it have been there on the plains of the southern Pampas? No. On the windswept Isle of Tierra del Huego—no, not there. In the humid jungles of northern Argentina? *Ahhh, yes!* While on their way to climb the famous X-spire, they had stumbled upon an ancient temple. Etched in the steps of the stone alter was a carving exactly like the one upon which their gaze was fixed this day. Somehow, here in El Arrgun, the pictograph cut into a basalt cliff seemed out of place. Yet, due to the almost mystic appearance and disappearance of Vern the wanderer, they did not doubt for a moment the authenticity of the carving—nor the meaning encrypted in the ancient stones.

Yes, the outline of a boat was obvious, and upon further inspection there was the figure of a person—a man of heroic stature with a great crested helmet, a soldier of fortune standing at the helm of a boat with a sword raised to the sky. Xavier stepped back for a better analysis of the wall carving. Suddenly, his sturdy frame was jolted, and he gasped. His thoughts cleared. While delving in a forbidden manuscript kept locked in a cellar vault in a cathedral where monks had tutored him as a young boy, Xavier remembers seeing an identical picture of an adventurer.

The name of the man was Rodrigo de Madrónna. He was an illustrious conquistador of Spain. He had thoroughly looted and burned multitudes of pagan cities of the South Land, sending to sea innumerable ships laden with gold and silver bound for the Port of Cádiz. It has been said that he once found a treasure cache of gold so immense it took six thousand native slaves a year to carry the hoard of wealth to the coast.

But still, Rodrigo was not satisfied. He pushed inland, delving low, and searching high, until *one* day, he found it! The condor's egg, a giant spherical jewel, larger and brighter than any known crystal ever seen by civilized man— even to this day. Rodrigo was a man of duty, forever bound to the service and glory of his king and country, yet the spherical jewel emitted a strange force which would not permit him to part with it.

The king of Spain, hearing of the marvelous jewel, commanded that Rodrigo de Madronna give it up. He refused. The church declared that they should have the mystical orb, and so they called upon Rodrigo to surrender it to the church. He refused again! Señor de Madrónna was then declared to be in league with the devil, and excommunicated from the church. The king, and the church wrote a decree for all the people of the land to obey. Señor de Madrónna's family name was to be stricken from all known records, and no tongue was ever allowed to mention the name *de Madrónna* again—on pain of death.

And so he fled, up the Pacific coast to the land of El Arrgun, then leagues further to a place known as the Queen of Rivers, stopping occasionally along the way to leave cryptic clues carved on stone outcrops at places like Neakhanie Mountain. Inland along the Queen of Rivers he fled. Of the carvings he left behind, etched in the rock outcrops, the boat always showed the helmeted figure of Rodrigo holding the condor's egg in one hand, and a sword in the other, pointing to a new direction.

Xavier is stirred from his thoughts by the screeching of a raven circling overhead. He remembered his meeting with Vern, and sensed that the long years of exile now have meaning—there is a greater purpose for he and Niguel. They are to be the seekers of the ancient orb said to have mysterious and extraordinary powers. To return to their homeland of Argentina with the condor's egg would surely restore their long lost honor.

Xavier could imagine Paola, the fat little monk, reminding him of the duties of gentlemanry, and the obligations of church, and of country, family, and honor. Returning the egg was to become his obsession, but first—he must find it. There must be another clue.

Just then, Niguel, absent mindedly brushed a large piece of moss off the rock adjacent to the boat pictograph. And there it was!—an additional clue to the carving, the likes of which they have never seen before. It appears to be the likeness of a mountain—but, No—a pinnacle!

"But, why a pinnacle," Niguel queries to himself. Xavier is amazed, and enlightened. How obvious it all is now. Where else would a condor make its nest, but on the summit of a pinnacle.

Niguel added, "...then, we should climb the pinnacle," stated as a suggestion rather than a fact, for Niguel knows his place. Xavier jumps up, slaps Niguel on the back, and with a smile on his face, says, "You are so right, my friend."

"But, which *one*, Señor Masters? For the carving does not indicate which one."

"Then, we should climb them all!" Xavier exclaims. "After all, there can only be several hundred, or so. Besides, we might get lucky after the first fifty."

And, so it was to be. One pinnacle, two pinnacle, three...twenty-three ...fifty...fifty-three, and so on—knowing that each summit climbed was one less summit to conquer until they would find the crystalline orb. The mysterious egg would be there, waiting for Xavier and Niguel, sparkling like a jewel.

The gauchos searched ardently for days without a moment of rest, but the days turned into weeks, and the weeks turned slowly into months. Undaunted by difficulties they ventured on. A year passed by and still they searched earnestly for the great orb. Where could it be?

After adhering to other cryptic clues of the ship carving left by Rodrigo de Madrónna, they ventured south east to an unknown corner of El Arrgun, into the heart of a sunbaked gulch in search of their destiny. Deep in the recesses of a desolate and untrammeled byway, as hungry vultures patiently perch in nearby juniper trees, another clue to the great puzzle was near—Xavier was certain of it!—and he was right.

It was a hot August afternoon, deep in a narrow canyon when suddenly their progress came to halt before an unusual tree, a juniper tree in fact, with a distinct triple split trunk that joins together a little higher into *one* tree. Here in this silent, dry corner in the desert of reason, they had found another clue.

A fly *buzzzzzz*'d around his head, intent upon biting at his rich blood. He twitched nervously, swatting at the annoying speck. Xavier surveyed the terrain ahead of him. "Extreme, and desolate," he muttered to himself. But it was not *too* extreme, of that he was certain, for the next clue left one hundred and fifty years before by the conquistidor Rodrigo de Madrónna was here. Hidden in the midst of this wind blown desert of sand, salt and sage, in a valley encircled by rimrock walls, near a rattlesnake home. It was here where the coyote roam, where moonless nights etch eternal eons in an empty space in time. Near the sweet scent of the ageless juniper tree—low and behold, what did Xavier see?

He stood gallently facing his future, erect upon his horse in magestic

Argentine form, a black narrow rimmed hat pulled low over his brow, and a *facón* dagger tucked in his belt. He was a man of dignity, and a man of bearing, knowing very well the reason for the hunt. He nudged the horse forward. Niguel was certain a great moment was near at hand.

The heat of a glaring sun beat down. Beads of sweat trickled past Xavier's temple down to his open coller. He scrutinizes the narrow ravine ahead of him, then peers at a scrap of diary which he holds in his hand. The diary is a secret quote of words from an old dusty book written countless years before by a desert wild man known as *"little Nikki"*.

He looks at the terrain around him once more, then compares the characteristics of the dry gulch with the words found in the old book. He lifts the diary closer to his nose, pondering the words and a rough sketch drawing, muttering to himself in a dry raspy voice. He licks his parched lips. "Well, indeed!" His thoughts clear and his countenance straightens—he smiles, and slowly turns to Niguel who is following close behind. *"Ahh*, my friend, follow me—for we have found him."

Xavier gently prods his horse forward and turns a crook in the narrow canyon. The gorge opens to a wide grassy dale. A small rustic shack stands next to the shaded recess of a steep wall at the head of the canyon. An inviting stream of water pours from a dark cleft in the rock cliff and meanders several meters to a pool of calm water. From there the waters submerge into the arid desert soil. Near the cabin a stout sycamore tree, full of leaf, spreads a canopy of shade over the cabin. There under the tree, in a wooden rocking chair was a hermit, relaxing in the cool of the shade, letting the heat of the day pass by. The hermit was intently reading from a *Book*, but looks up when he hears Xavier and Niguel draw near. He smiles and waves to them, heralding the two gauchos to come near. And so they did.

Finally after months of searching throughout the desert country, Xavier had stumbled upon the secret abode of the wanderer *little Nikki*. Long silent years had elapsed since any person had seen Nikki, for he had become thoroughly engrossed in searching for the egg of the condor ever since the end of the Great War. Yes, he was getting on in years, a little grey in the beard, a slight stoop and a limp that required a walking staff, but overall he was still a well tanned sturdy man with an intense gaze. With eagerness Xavier struck up a conversation. It was like two old friends from long ago meeting again to talk about their adventures. Wild stories of their homeland were mingled with stories from the new country. That day was the best of times, and will long be remembered by Xavier and Niguel. Yes, Nikki's clothes were a bit haggard from years of heavy use, and his thoughts wandered a little bit, but Xavier overlooked every fault because he was blueblooded kin.

Xavier and Niguel were captivated by the desert hermit as he talked of extreme climbs and wild adventures. The gauchos ears were pricked to a heighthened degree as Nikki told stories of ascending many great summits, and of harrowing escapes from the clutches of death. Nikki filled the gauchos heads with plans to destinations unknown, of clues that led elsewhere away from the great pinnacles where the condor's egg should be. In a small way Nikki was suggesting to Xavier that other things were just as important. But Xavier sensed he was holding back—there was something he would not tell. Why else did he travel to Patagonia for a second time seven years ago.

You see, my friend, little Nikki was interested in *birds*, too. In fact, both he and his lovely esposa vacationed down to the old country for a while. Xavier believed there was more than just birds on Nikki's thoughts during that Patagonian vacation. There was something Nikki was not telling Xavier. Had he searched through old manuscripts for another clue to the mysterious orb? Had he overstepped an all important sign somewhere along the way, then retraced his steps to be sure? All the summits, and all the secrets up until now had failed to reveal to Nikki the whereabouts of the elusive condor's egg.

Late that night, while Nikki was out tending to his burro, Xavier and Niguel inadvertently glanced at an open diary laying on the table in the one room shack. Pages of inky scribble unveiled years of fruitless searching for the condor's egg. There was even a detailed summary of where he believed the egg to be hidden. The diary described how he and his beloved esposa, and their trusty burro had wandered for years throughout the highlands of El Arrgun in search of that one summit certain to hold the egg.

Nikki had become frustrated attempting to solve the riddle of the mysterious orb—that is, until their vacation a few years ago to the old country. While searching through a dusty manuscript in an ancient monastery in Patagonia he began to see the light, he rediscovered vital information he had previously overlooked. Condor's seldom lay their eggs on summits, but rather they would roll or push the egg into small openings or caves high up on isolated cliffs. So Nikki and his beloved esposa started afresh, and put all their energy and passion into the search for the crystalline orb by inspecting every cavity, clevage, and cave in El Arrgun.

Xavier and Niguel stayed on for a nearly a month, waiting for the heat of summer to ease before venturing forth again on their quest. Nikki told countless epics to his captive audience. He even whispered ideas of an imminent triumph into the alert ears of Xavier and Niguel. He kept insisting that the answer to the mysterious orb lay in *another* direction. Xavier pondered and reasoned with Nikki. The desert hermits ideas were sound, yet a haunting certainty in Xavier's conscience assured him the answer to the grand mystery lay hidden high on a summit elsewhere.

One fact was certain to Xavier. Every summit Nikki had explored was eggless. The only problem—Nikki would not tell *which* pinnacles he had been on!

Xavier suspected that minions dedicated to Nikki were everywhere. Each day some of his followers would look in caves high upon craggy cliffs while others searched for the condor's egg on cold, wind swept summits—searching, and still searching.

As Xavier and Niguel rode away on their horses, little Nikki kept rambling on about the birds. "Birds, birds," he kept saying as he slowly twisted his long handlebar mustache between his fingers. "Do you have any idea how many *terns* there are out there?"

After several more years of searching on summits and *in caves* for the condor's egg, Xavier and Niguel return to little Nikki's desert rancho, with the hope that he might give further clues as to the whereabouts of the crystalline orb.

There beneath the broad sweeping branches of the sycamore tree, the three adventurers relaxed for a spell, swapping illustrious stories few people will ever hear. Tales of strange places and exotic lands could be heard, like Xavier's continental journey along the great divide, and of Nikki's scrambles through desert canyon passages. Niguel even told of meeting close kin in the heart of Bolivia, when the land was still torn by the turmoil of war.

One day, when humid air hung like a thick woolen garment around the rancho, Nikki's countenance changed. A deep, troubling thought creased his brow. His voice lowered. A vise of heavy silence gripped the air, not a breath was heard. Nikki leaned close to Xavier and Niguel, and in a whispered tone uttered these penetrating words, "There are a few more turns which I have not told you—there is something you need to know."

In all the hours of meaningful discussion between Nikki and Xavier, he had never revealed such thoughts as these from the depth of his soul. The whispered message readily pricked Xavier and Niguels ears, and for just a moment Xavier misinterpreted Nikki's words. "Little Nikki—my dear friend," Xavier responds with kindness, not intending to disappoint, "We are not interested in birds."

"*Ahh!* But Xavier, this has nothing to do with *terns*! This has everything to do with your quest—your destiny. I have felt a strong kindred spirit toward you and Niguel, and now I wish to reveal to you a secret." He continued. "I am an old man now, unable to pursue my dreams with vigor. I would like you to—*well*,tomorrow my friend, pack your bags and be ready—we leave at dawn." He got up from his rocking chair and turned away from their presence, and entered the darkness of the cabin without speaking another word.

Later that evening Xavier pondered immense thoughts while resting under the majestic sycamore tree. "What does this tree know of destiny?" he pondered. "What is Nikki's secret—what does he truly see?"

In the darkness before dawn they rode out across the plain, over dry and hostile land fraught with narrow twisted gulches and ash colored sage. This barren, nameless place in the heart of El Arrgun is serious business for the foolhardy, but to these Patagonian adventurers it is a place to be reckoned with. "Here we face the challenge," said Xavier.

Soon the landscape became flat and bleak as far as the eye could see. They had come to the dreaded alkaline desert which Nikki said must be traversed in order to reach their destination. Boldly they marched into the desert, into a sea of sweltering heat. Lakes of watery aberration beckoned elusively to the men. Each day the bulging water bags that were strapped to the horses shrunk until they were soon dry and empty. Yet Xavier was not seeing watery illusions. Rather he was charged with a Masters family zeal, impassioned to his very soul with the hunt for the crystalline orb hidden long ago by Señor Madrónna.

From the east a vengence driven sandstorm hurled clouds of stinging sand upon the travelers. While Nikki and Xavier fought to see mere meters ahead into the storm, Niguel enviously wished for easier times in the old country where fresh guavas and papayas were plentiful, foods which he relished to taste right now. The storm abated, yet the intense desert heat like a brick continued to press hard upon the three riders as they crossed the alkaline flats. Under stressful moments like these tense nerves have been known to unravel, and this adventure with Nikki was beginning to get on Xaviers nerves. Was it all an illusion? Was this desert just a wretched dream?

But *low!* Five days out on the dust choked trail Nikki guides the weary men to a hidden spring of refreshing water pouring from a cleft of rock. They gladly refilled the water bags, and rested for a short spell before setting out again.

High above the desert floor buzzards slowly circle on the air thermals. Anticipating an easy meal, the buzzards keep a watchful eye on the three adventurers, especially the *large one* on the big horse. Having soared high above many meals similar to this one, the buzzards were certain of a feast-in-the-making this time, as well. For they could smell rich *imported* blood, the blood of Xavier, and were willing to ride the wind currents for days just to feast on his wealth. *Ahh!* But the vultures did not know the perseverance of Xavier, for he is willing to risk it all, even the lack of food and water, just to have the crystal.

During their journey they rode past great heaps of white fossilized mammoth bones and tusks. The bones, of course, were of no interest to these adventurers for they had more important matters to which *they* must attend.

Up into the grand mountain range they traveled, away from the desert heat. Nikki became suspicious and sensitive as the men rode higher. He twitched frequently, analyzing each crook and turn in the trail ahead while nervously peering behind to see if anyone was following. To the left he urged his horse rapidly on a false lead then back to the right, as if searching—but for what?

Curled up on a rock a rattlesnake suddenly spooks the horses, sending riders and their beasts bucking in three different directions. Each rider struggles for several moments to bring his beast under control. Little Nikki, unnerved a bit by all the ruckus, curses and spits tobacco at the snake. Xavier, in the moment of excitement has chewed off the end of his soggy cigar. Niguel of course, was more concerned about where they would stop for their next meal, while Boomba merely barked and wagged his tail at all the nonsense. In the distance coyotes howl from a rimrock cliff. Xavier is sufficiently certain the coyotes are laughing at him. Boomba replies with a mournful song in return, for they are distant relatives of his, you know.

The mood of the moment on this momentous August day reminds Xavier of his adventures in the old country, but there is no time to reminisce about those days now, so the three horsemen move on toward their destiny. High in the western sky brilliant shafts of light pierce through the trees as each delicate ray dances upon the needle covered forest floor. Here amidst the silent breath of solitude, is a sweet whispered scent of a cool summers breeze. Greatness is near—somewhere, very near...and Xavier perceives it, as the energy rebounds in his Patagonian bones.

But suddenly, little Nikki stops. He dismounts from his burro and silently prepares for camp. Xavier and Niguel, confused by the abrupt change in plan follow suit and dismount from their steeds to help set up camp. All the while, a plague of unanswered questions remained, questions they wished to ask Nikki but would not. Are we near the next clue? Did Nikki find the mysterious ship? Will we meet an infamous person—or perhaps, find the fabulous orb itself! Could it be possible?

Niguel dutifully applies himself to the task of gathering wood for a small fire, then fills a pot of water to boil for yerba mate. Xavier unsaddles the horses, then looses them so they may wander freely in the nearby glades for tender grasses to feed on. As Xavier returns to camp he stops abruptly, suspicion creases his brow—he peers over at Niguel. Niguel, sensing something amiss as well, turns from his campfire duties and looks up at Xavier. Suddenly, both men stiffen, their eyes open wide—Nikki is *gone*! One moment the man is here silently preparing camp, and then, in the next moment, like vapor, he has vanished.

With a sense of duty and concern for his comrade Xavier reaches for his machete. Niguel, bound by a life long duty to assist the Masters family in all business affairs immediately steps forward with his machete in hand. Quickly the two men move up hill searching for a clue as to the whereabouts of Nikki. Boomba doing his dog duty tracks a wide zigzagging pattern in front of the men. Soon, the ponderosa forest thins, and a tall, menacing scarp of gray basalt rim rock, hundreds of meters high halts their progress. Boomba sniffs a hot scent over to the right. Could it be Nikki's? Stirred by the intrigue of mystery Xavier and Niguel hasten along the cliff base in search of their missing comrade. Where could he be? What could have happened?

Ahead near a tangle of vine maple a dark recess in the rim rock cliff beckons to the men. Upon closer inspection they discover a great cavernous entrance. Boomba, inquisitive till now, stops at a line that separates the sunlight from the darkness, unwilling to step beyond. Xavier glances at Niguel and at Boomba, then leans forward slightly, shading his eyes with a hand, straining to see beyond the light into the darkness. Cold air flows from the cave, whispering as it passes by Xavier. He presses forward against the cold airmass, straining to see into the darkness, but still he cannot see. Xavier quickly analyzes the situation only to realize he must step forward to find out what is in there. He moves slowly from the light into the caves darkness with Niguel and Boomba following.

A rattlesnake slithers away into a tiny dusty corner. Scorpions, offended by the arrival of the unwelcome intruders scurry into their nooks. Faint boot prints on the dusty floor in front of the men, lead inward into the blackness. The prints are Nikki's. Xavier clears his throat, "*Mmnn*—Nikki? Silence. With a stronger tone he speaks again, "Nikki, are you there?" Hollow words echo upon the cavern wall, but afterward only silence remains. Not even the drop of bat guano plumbs the depths of this eeriness.

Xaviers eyes adjust to the darkness...shapes and shadows begin to appear. He holsters the machete, yet keeps a firm grip on the ivory hilt, just in case. Being strengthened by the fact that he can now see in this darkness, Xavier, with his curiosity piqued to find the answer as to this mysterious cave, breathes deep, pulls in his chin and walks into the inner darkness. Niguel and Boomba step forward as well. The cavern, stays small for one hundred meters, before opening up into a large amphitheater. High in the ceiling of this chamber is a small opening where the light of the outside world breaks through, sending a thin shaft of dusty light piercing down downward at an angle to the cavern floor, illuminating the cavern in a dim gray light.

At the center of the great cavern, behind where the shaft of light touches the floor, a great carved stone obelisk several meters in height, stands erect. In front of the obelisk a large rectangular stone chamber dominates the room. Xavier is drawn to this obelisk, and especially the stone chamber. He has not seen anything like this since the jungles of Argentina, and even then it was not as mysteriously captivating as this place. He peers around the cavern at a jumble of boulders and blocky steps. On the rocky ledges a glint of color sparkles in his eye. The reflection of color is of steel and gold.

Gold! Xavier's heart leaps a beat at the very thought of the word, for gold is nearly as elusive as the crystalline orb, and almost as precious, too. Yes, along the walls of the great chamber were pikes, swords, conquistador helmets, and gilded crest plates, stacked neatly and standing at readiness, silently facing the great monolith of stone in the center of the room as if waiting for immenent return of the master. But deep inside his heart Xavier senses that that will never be.

Clink. A sound! To the right, there amidst a cluster of conquistadorian armor is Little Nikki, sitting with a gold helmet on his head. He grins sheepishly at Xavier momentarily, then straightens his composure. Nikki, in a small voice says, "Welcome, Xavier—and you too, Niguel. As you are guessing right now, the rock upon which you are now looking is indeed—*rrmmnn...*" Nikki clears his throat, then speaks louder with a low echoing voice, "...the tomb of Rodrigo de Madrónna."

Aghast at Nikki's words of revelation, Xavier speechlessly stares at Nikki, then looks back upon the obelisk and tomb. For years Xavier has been captivated both day and night by this legendary man of mystery—de Madrónna. Held prisoner by the eminence of a nobleman whom he had never met in person, Xavier has always felt strong kinsmanship ties to de Madrónna. The very *name* evokes respect, even from the breath of Xavier. He silently whispers, "de Madrónna...de Madrónna..."

After all these years Xavier finally stands in the presence of the great *master.* He studies the monolith, then steps forward—slowly. Niguel remains still, as does Boomba, both taking in the scene of the meeting of these two great persons, something few people ever really see. A tear wells up in Niguel's eye at the sight of this reunion.

Xavier reaches out and touches the edge of the massive headstone and sarcophagus, almost expecting a curse to occur and the walls of the cave to come crashing down, but there is only peace. He grips the edge of the tomb lid, then looks up at the pictographic symbols and Latin etchings cut into the stone surface. Xavier, captivated by the tomb grasps the lid firmly and pushes the lid aside and peers into the recess. Inside lay the white bones of a man wearing a gold conquistadorian breastplate. A gold helmet and a steel embossed straight sword lay next to the skeleton. On the gold breastplate, set amidst a pattern of ornate acorns and oak leaves were the exquisitely etched letters, *R de M.*

The drums of eternity rolled heavy upon the ears of Xavier as he stares at the letters. He had never imagined that all the frustrating years of searching would lead here. He peers up at the headstone with a perplexed and saddened gaze. Gradually he focuses on the Latin words enscripted on the headstone. He has not used his Latin in years, but the symbol and the words are quite legible, even in the dim lighting of the cave. The symbol is obvious—it is the sign of the crystal, an elongated diamond. The chiseled inscription below the symbol read:

MADRÓNNA
For the glory of the hunt
Because it is there

Xavier's movements captivate Niguel and Nikki. Confused, and agitated by the mysterious words Xavier utters, "Because it is there?" Xavier rumbles with anger at the unreasonable nature of the words etched on the stone obelisk. "Yes—*yes!* Blast you Señor Madrónna." The cavern walls echo the name in return. "Where—I demand that you show me *where* it is!"

Little Nikki chuckles humorously to himself upon seeing Xavier's outpouring of emotion focused upon a pillar of unspeakable stone and pile of bones laying in a sarcophagus. When youth vigorously marching forward without insight, *oh* what a dry desert of reason it can be. Nikki stands up, and walks over to Xavier.

"Xavier—*Xavier*, my dear friend, Xavier. Come now, Señor Masters. Do you not understand all that you see, even now? There really is no condor's egg. Madrónna was a searcher in a brave new world, a man of immense stature who conquered the unknown in a time long ago. He was a man who charted the great unknown in search of excitement and adventure."

Xavier eyes Nikki with intense thought. Is Nikki suggesting that Madrónna was out for the adventure? Not possible! Is it?

Nikki continues, "Madrónna lived for his king and country in his early years, but later when his eyes were opened, he lived for another reason. The world was not big enough to appease Madrónna, until he found *something* greater than a mere crystal. He found greatness in truth, and honor. He wanted his followers to understand this secret, as well, but only after they traveled long enough would they begin to see. Do you, Xavier? It was all a game by Señor de Madrónna."

Xavier shook his head, astounded at the words of Nikki. "No, this cannot possibly be!" Again little Nikki responds, "Have you learned nothing on all your journeys? Have you gained nothing from your grand expeditions? But I say again, Xavier, you have learned something! You have learned truth, honesty, patience, and perseverance—these are all the true values, the real virtues which you have found through your search, as all good friends must do. You have learned of pain, suffering, thirst, starvation...lessons learned by the experience of insight. Recognize what you have found."

"This journey is what you make of it, not what it makes of you. Will you be disappointed, even now after all that you have seen. Do you not realize, do you not see the treasure you have gained, something which cannot be taken from you. The orb is not a *tangible* thing. You have indeed found, and found well, Xavier Masters!"

"*No—no*, it cannot be!" Xavier turns away from Nikki, refusing to believe the possibility. In a deep provoking moment of solitude he quietly faces the tomb and obelisk, then pulls the tomb lid closed. He looks up at the words on the headstone, and mumbles something under his breath. He turns to his compatriots and says, "We are privelaged to meet the great Senor de Madrónna, and have looked upon all this splendor, but we will leave everything as it is." Like silent thistles pricking his conscious, deep unanswered questions remained, but no further words were spoken that day. So the men turned away from the presence of the honorable Madrónna, and walked back to the entrance of the cave, to a brilliant shining light of a late afternoon sun.

Yes, it is true, in time—a year, or two, or four from now, long after their departure from Nikki's rancho, only then does Xavier come around to believing Little Nikki's words. But on this particular day deep in the dark cavernous tomb of Señor de Madrónna, he remains certain of his search to find that grand and elusive orb, convinced that the crystalline condor's egg is out there somewhere.

Little Nikki, in his later years sits in a rocking chair under the majestic sycamore tree at his desert rancho, quietly enjoying the beauty of the land, listening to the call of the birds, and especially the *terns*. He breathes in the sweet pine smell of the ponderosa, and the spicey odor of the juniper tree. He writes letters to friends in far away places, even to friends on the Pampas of Argentina.

Nikki thoroughly enjoys meeting old compatriots, friends who occasionally stop by for a visit now and then, to tell of their grand adventures, friends who also speak admirably of Xavier and Niguel, and Boomba, too. To Nikki the company of others is indispensable, because to Nikki the orb does not exist anymore. The condor's egg is only an imaginary tool of Rodrigo de Madrónna, a right of passage, where in some people like the king and the church, it brought out only the worst, while in others like Xavier and Niguel, it brought out only the best.

Seven galloping steeds,
Blaze 'cross the fertile Pampas plain,
To the west stand majestic sentinels,
Towers of Tyme and Payne,
A millennium has carved magnificent lines,
Storms have etched their name,
Patagonian peaks of honor and truth,
Have no place for shame,
Young maverick gauchos, who travel far and near,
Xavier and Niguel venture to the height so sheer,
What can quench their zeal, What can slow their pace?
Fearless are these men who leave but little trace,
Pass the silver piton, no shadows in the dust,
In artificial rules they hold no faith or trust,
Of these gallant gauchos their lives are full of song,
Brave is the valor of these fighting men, strong,
Land of Argentina, breathlessly my choice,
Homeland of my father, I long to hear your voice,
Temperate plain, worth your weight in gold,
Surround me with your cattle herds like a grazing fold,
Lush vale of Pampas grass, lofty windswept knoll,
Here breeds the cleansing of my veins,
Graze on, graze on, eternal gaucho soul.

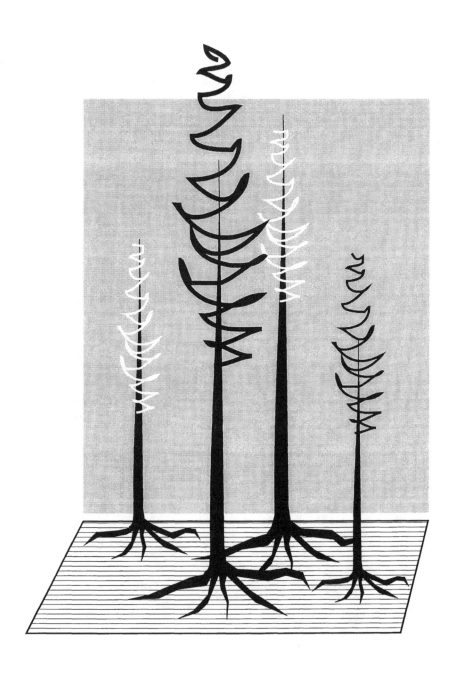

Appendix: I

Climbing History

This appendix lists FA data for most of the climbs in this book. A special thanks to all of you who freely shared your part of this analogy. The occasional blank space simply indicates information that was unavailable at the time of publishing. There are bound to be errors in this guide. I hope that the errors found will be of little significance.

The following definitions will help readers to interpret the first ascent data:

FA (First Ascent): Aid ascent, attempted free ascent, or an ascent.

FFA (First Free Ascent): Free ascent with NO tension, weighting of pro or falls.

FRA (First Recorded Ascent): It is likely that the climb was done previously, but no record exists as to who did it.

TR (Top-rope): Climbing a route with a safety line that is anchored from above.

GFA (Ground-up First Ascent): Without pre-inspection.

BROUGHTON BLUFF

North Face

1. **Traffic Court** FFA (before) 8-87 Wayne Wallace, Robert McGown (ascent after collapse) 8-22-92 Tim Olson
2. **G. G. Variation**
3. **Gandalf's Grip** GFA (regular route) 1968 Steve Strauch, Jim O'Connell FFA (by variation) 9-28-69 Steve Strauch, John Hack
4. **New Wave** FFA 1st pitch 7-87 R. McGown, W. Wallace
5. **Peach Cling** GFA 1972 Jim Mayers, Gail Van Hoorn FFA summer 1978 Doug Bower and partner
6. **Cindyrella** FFA 7-24-93 Steve Elder
7. **Risky Business** FA 7-87 W. Wallace, R. McGown
8. **Reckless Driver** FFA 1st and 2nd pitch 2-7-87 T. Olson FFA Complete (1,2,3) 7-15-87 W. Wallace, R. McGown
9. **Sweet Emotion** FA 8-87 W. Wallace, R. McGown
10. **American Graffiti** FA 10-87 W. Wallace

Hanging Gardens Wall - Left Half

1. **Giants Staircase** FA Unknown
2. **Edges and Ledges** FFA 8-92 Greg Murray
3. **The Sickle** FRA 1972 Ancil Nance
4. **The Hammer** FA Unknown
5. **Prometheus Slab** FA 1965 Bob Waring, John Wells, Bruce Holcomb
6. **Spud** FA Unknown
7. **Tip City** FA 1979 Jim Olson, Jay Kerr
8. **Lean Years** FA Unknown

9. **Hangover** (TR) 1979 J. Kerr, J. Olson
10. **Chockstone Chimney** GFA 1965 B. Waring, J. Wells, B. Holcomb
11. **Milestone** FA Unknown

Hanging Gardens Wall - Right Half
12. **Loose Block Overhang** Probable FFA 1975 Monty Mayko, Jim Garrett
13. **Grace and Danger** FFA 6-30-91 Dave Sowerby
14. **Slapfest** FFA 1-12-92 T. Olson, Cindy Long
15. **Least Resistance** FRA 1971 T. Bielefeldt, Tim Carpenter, Bruce Weideman
    FFA Fall 1975 Roger Baker
16. **Dynamic Resistance** FFA 7-9-88 W. Wallace, R. McGown
17. **Sandy's Direct** FFA 1977 R. McGown, Mike Smelsar, Sandy Regan
18. **Face Not Friction** GFA 1975 Alan Campbell and partner
    FFA 5-30-81 Mark Cartier
19. **Hanging Gardens** GFA 1965 B. Waring, J. Wells, B. Holcomb
    FRFA 1974 Rich Borich
20. **BFD** FFA 1975 Bruce Casey, M. Mayko
21. **Mr. Potato** GFA 1973 A. Campbell and partner
    FFA 7-18-81 B. Casey, Jeff Thomas
22. **From Something to Nothing** FFA 10-11-87 W. Wallace, T. Olson
23. **Fun in the Mud** FA 1977 R. McGown, Terry Yates
24. **Circus Act** FFA 9-19-87 W. Wallace, T. Olson
25. **Shining Star** FA 1977 Mike Smelsar, R. McGown
    FFA complete 3-16-87 R. McGown, W. Wallace
26. **Hung Jury** FFA 5-87 R. McGown, W. Wallace
27. **Hang 'Em High** FFA 9-7-87 R. McGown, W. Wallace
28. **Main Vein** FFA 8-91 Chuck Buzzard, Steve Mrazek
29. **Sesame Street** GFA 1972 A. Campbell, Gail Van Hoorn
    FFA 7-8-73 Dean Fry and partner
30. **Demian** GFA Fall 1976 R. McGown, M. Smelsar
    FFA Unknown
31. **Endless Sleep** GFA Spring 1977 R. McGown, M. Smelsar
32. **Peer Pressure** GFA 1972 or 73 J. Mayers, A. Campbell
    FFA Spring 1977 M. Smelsar, R. McGown
33. **Scorpion Seams** GFA 1980 R. McGown, Steve Hillanger, Mike Corning
    FFA Alex Russell 8-7-96, other variation FFA Gary Rall 7-11-93
34. **Black Prow** FA 1979 R. McGown, M. Simpson
    FFA D. Sowerby 6-18-94

Red Wall
1. **Arch De Triumph** FA 1987 W. Wallace
2. **Arcturas**
3. **Anastasia**
4. **Dry Bones**

5. **On The Loose** FFA 1978 R. McGown
6. _____ TR Greg Lyon
7. **Classic Crack** FA and FFA Unknown
    TR Free in 1972 by J. Mayers. Led Free in 1975 by Doug Bower
8. **Thai Stick** FA 1979 R. McGown
9. **Mr. Bentley** TR 1981 Ed Welter, Jack Goble
10. **Sheer Stress** GFA 1974 A. Campbell and partner
    FFA complete 1975 Charlie Priest, Charlie Martin
11. **Physical Graffiti** FA Summer 1977 R. McGown, M. Smelsar
    FFA Summer 1977 D. Bower and partner
12. **Habitual Ritual** FFA 2-5-92 Gary Rall
13. **Physical Direct** FFA 11-18-90 T. Olson, Cecil Colley
14. **Hit the Highway** FA 1977 B. Casey, M. Mayko
15. **Kashmir** FFA (via Classic Crack) 11-18-90 G. Rall
16. **Red Eye** FFA 1st pitch 1976 M. Mayko, B. Casey
    FA complete 1978 M. Cartier and partner
    FFA 10-3-78 J. Thomas, Paul Gleeson
17. **Critical Mass** FFA Summer 1981 R. McGown, Scott Woolums
    Retro bolt ascent on 9-5-90 by G. Rall
18. **E. Pluribus Pinhead** FFA 8-91 S. Mrazek, C. Buzzard
19. **Opus (Direct Start)** FFA 2-5-92 D. Sowerby
20. **Sheer Energy** GFA Fall 1979 Jim Olson or Alan Kearney
21.
22. **Hard Body** FFA 5-5-91 T. Olson, W. Wallace
23. **Shoot from the Hip** FFA 4-7-91 T. Olson
24. **No Friction** FA 7-88 W. Wallace
25. **That's the Way** FA 7-88 W. Wallace

Bridge Cliff
1. **Under Your Belt** FA 4-24-87 W. Wallace, Scott Tracy
2. **Walk on the Wild Side** GFA 1977 Jay Kerr, David Howe
3. **Edge of Eternity** FFA 2-25-88 W. Wallace, R. McGown, T. Olson
4. **Spidermonkey** GFA 1977 R. McGown, M. Simpson
5. **Fruit Bat** GFA 1977 R. McGown, D. Bower
6. **Seventh Sojourn** FA 1977 R. McGown, M. Simpson, Roger Baker
7. **Shandor** FA 1-8-88 W. Wallace
⊗. **Eagle's Wing** FFA 3-6-93 D. Sowerby

Spring Rock
1. **Toe Cleavage** FFA 11-6-87 W. Wallace
2. **Velcro Fly** FFA 4-9-89 T. Olson, W. Wallace
3. **Free Bird** FFA 11-8-87 W. Wallace
4. **Ground Effects** FFA Summer 1989 G. Lyon
5. **Jumping Jack Thrash** (TR) 10-86 J. Goble, E. Welter, M. Cartier
    FFA 9-5-90 G. Rall

6. **The Spring** GFA 1977 R. McGown, B. Casey
7. **Short Fuse** FFA 6-28-92 T. and C. Olson
8. **Dyno-Mite** FFA 11-27-87 W. Wallace
⊗. **Short Circuit** FFA 3-28-93 Andrew Glasfeld

Bat Wall
1. **Hanging Tree** FA 6-2-77 R. McGown, J. Thomas
2. **Go Back to the Gym** GFA 10-28-90 W. Wallace, T. Olson
3. **Dracula** FA Unknown
   FFA 5-20-90 G. Rall
4. **Bela Lugosi** FFA 9-16-90 G. Rall
5. **Fright Night** FFA 7-12-91 Matthias Pausch
6. **The Haunting** GFA 1977 B. Casey, M. Mayko
   FFA 1-2-92 G. Rall
7. **Bad Omen** (got the horse for my saddle) FFA 12-16-90 T. Olson
8. **Danse Macabre** FFA 8-19-92 D. Sowerby
9. **Bloodsucker** GFA Summer 1977 R. McGown, M. Smelsar
   FFA 1-20-92 Jay Green
10. **Bloodline** GFA 2-91 W. Wallace, R. McGown
    FFA 1-19-92 D. Sowerby
11. **Predator** FFA 10-16-93 D. Sowerby
12. **Superstition** GFA 1977 R. McGown, S. Woolums, J. Olson
    FFA 7-11-81 J. Thomas, M. Cartier
13. **Lost Boys** FA Unknown
    FFA complete 12-2-90 W. Wallace, T. Olson, Jay Green, Mike Cartier
14. **Mystic Pizza** FFA 12-9-90 W. Wallace, T. Olson
15. **Mystic Void** FA 1977 R. McGown, S. Woolums
16. **Well Hung** GFA 1977 R. McGown, M. Simpson
    FFA Unknown
17. **Gold Arch** GFA 1978 R. McGown, D. Bower, T. Yates
18. **The Hunger** FFA 8-29-92 D. Sowerby
19. **Dark Shadows** GFA 1979 R. McGown, J. Olson, M. Simpson
    FFA 11-2-90 D. Sowerby, Mike Sessions
20.
21. **Manson Family Reunion** FA Unknown
    FFA 9-7-92 S. Mrazek
22. **Vampyr**
    FFA 9-26-94 D. Sowerby
23. **Remain in Light**
    FFA D. Sowerby 11-22-93
24.
25.

Trinity Wall
1. **Bust A Move** FFA 6-2-91 W. Wallace, T. Olson

2. **Father** FA 3-6-88 W. Wallace
   FFA 11-11-90 W. Wallace, T. Olson

Berlin Wall
1. **Closet Nazi** FFA 9-90 J. Green
2. **Recipe for Airtime** FA 1-29-95 T. Olson, Harry
3. **Twist and Crawl** FA Spring 1991 W. Wallace, T. Olson
   FFA 7-91 M. Carter
4. **Genocide** FA 1-7-95 D. Sowerby
5. **Pride and Joy** FFA 11-11-90 T. Olson, W. Wallace

Jungle Cliff
1. **Zimbabwe** GFA 9-29-91 D. Sowerby, Greg Carmichael
2. **Slash and Burn** GFA 3-23-91 W. Wallace, T. Olson
   FFA 11-7-92 D. Sowerby
3. **Under the Yum-Yum Tree** GFA 2-7-88 W. Wallace, G. Lyon
4. **Tarzan** FFA 3-13-92 D. Sowerby
5. **Crime Wave** FFA 6-13-92 T. and C. Olson
6. **Gorilla Love Affair** FFA 2-9-92 C. Long and T. Olson
7. **Out of Africa** GFA 7-79 S. Woolums, R. McGown
8. **Heart of Darkness** FFA 4-27-91 D. Sowerby
⊗. **Mowgli Direct** FFA 1-17-96 D. Sowerby
9. **Mowgli's Revenge** FFA 2-2-92 D. Sowerby
10. **Amazon Woman** GFA Fall 1991 W. Wallace, T. Olson
    FFA 1-17-92 Heather Macdonald, C. Long
11. **Amazon Man** GFA 7-79 R. McGown, Levi Grey, M. Simpson
12. **Killer Pygmy** GFA (to Skull Ledge) 11-30-91 W. Wallace, T. Olson
    GFA 2nd pitch 12-10-91 W. Wallace, R. McGown
13. **Mujahideen** GFA 11-27-87 W. Wallace

New Frontier Wall
1. **Luck of the Draw** FFA 10-9-93 Greg Murray
⊗. **Touch and Go** FFA 8-8-93 Greg Murray
2. **Alma Mater** FFA 6-2-91 W. Wallace, T. Olson
⊗. **Split Decision** FFA 8-27-93 Greg Murray
⊗. **Tin Star** FFA 9-6-93 Greg Murray
⊗. **True Grit** FFA 8-27-93 Greg Murray
⊗. **Pony Express** FFA 9-93 Greg Murray
3. **Happy Trails** FFA 1-2-91 D. Sowerby, Mike Smith
4. **Wild Wild West** GFFA 2-23-91 D. Sowerby, Ric Weaver, T. Olson
5. **Pioneer Spirit** FFA 8-18-91 D. Sowerby
6. **Promised Land** FFA 9-7-91 D. Sowerby
7.

ROCKY BUTTE

Poodle Pinnacle
1. **Poodle with a Mohawk** FFA 6-87 Gary Rall

Trivial Pinnacle
1. **Harlequin** FFA 8-9-87 T. Olson, R. McGown
2. **Trivial Pursuit** FA 8-9-87 R. McGown, T. Olson
3. **The Joker** FA Unknown

Silver Bullet Bluff
1. **Unknown**
2. **Captain She's Breaking Up** FA 8-87 R. McGown, Jim Mohel, T. Olson
3. **Unknown**
4. **Sundance Kid** FA Unknown
   FRFA 7-87 Greg Lyon, R. McGown, Chris McMullin
5. **Panama Red** FFA 7-87 G. Lyon, C. McMullin, R. McGown
6. **Miss Kitty** FA 7-87 R. McGown, Eric Simmons
7. **Gunsmoke** FFA 7-20-87 R. McGown, T. Olson
8. **Bite the Bullet** FFA 7-20-87 R. McGown, Wayne Wallace, T. Olson
9. **Jack of Hearts** FFA 7-15-87 W. Wallace, R. McGown, T. Olson
10. **Silver Bullet** FFA 7-20-87 R. McGown, T. Olson, Steve Wong
11. **Urban Cowboy** FFA 7-20-87 R. McGown, T. Olson, S. Wong
12. **Last Tango** FFA 7-87 R. McGown, T. Olson
13. **Fandango** FFA 7-13-87 R. McGown, T Olson
14. **Midnight Warrior** FFA 7-13-87 R. McGown, T Olson
15. **Superman Crack** FFA 7-25-87 R. McGown, T. Olson
16. **Centurion** FA 7-15-87 R. McGown, T. Olson
    FFA 7-87 W. Wallace, R. McGown
20. **Invisible Man** GFA 7-87 R. McGown, J. Mohel
21. **Temporary Arete** FFA 9-88 Ed and Vern Welter

Video Bluff
1. **Body Language** FFA 6-11-87 R. McGown, T. Olson
2. **Body Bionics** FFA 6-11-87 R. McGown, T. Olson
3. **Ace** FFA 6-6-87 Dan Wright, T. Olson
4. **Eve of Destruction** FFA 6-5-87 R. McGown, T. Olson, Jim Wright, Eve McDermitt
5. **Live Wire** FFA 6-5-87 R. McGown, T. Olson
6. **Damaged Circuit** FFA 6-5-87 R. McGown, T. Olson
7. **Robotics** FFA 6-6-87 T. Olson, D. Wright
8. **Edge of Might** FFA 8-87 Mike Pajunas, G. Rall
9. **Hard Contact** FFA 6-88 G. Lyon
10. **Lever or Leaver** FFA 8-87 M. Pajunas, G. Rall, John Sprecher
11. **Persistence of Time** FA Summer 1991 Chad Franklin
12. **Zeeva** FFA 8-20-82 T. Olson, D. Wright

13. **Flakey Old Man** FFA 5-29-87 T. Olson, R. McGown
14. **MTV**
15. **Stranger Than Friction** FFA 5-29-87 T. Olson, R. McGown
16. **Panes of Reality** FFA 5-29-87 R. McGown, T. Olson
17. **Stained Glass** FFA 5-29-87 T. Olson, R. McGown
18. **Toxic Waltz** FA 11-91 C. Franklin
19. **E-Z Corner** FA Unknown

Dream Weaver Wall
1. **Dream Weaver** FFA 4-86 M. Pajunas, R. Moody
2. **Head Bangers Ball** FFA 10-9-88 W. Wallace
3. **Tiger Pause** FFA 10-85 M. Pajunas, Joe Parsley

Wizard Wall
1. **Kleen Korner** FA Unknown
2. **Naked Savage** FFA 6-4-87 R. McGown, T. Olson
3. **Lord of the Jungle** FFA 6-2-87 R. McGown, T. Olson
4. **Slavemaker** FFA 6-4-87 R. McGown, T. Olson
5. **Grub** FFA 5-24-87 R. McGown, T. Olson
6. **Eye in the Sky** FFA 6-2-87 R. McGown, T. Olson
7. **Phylynx** (TR) 1987 Mike Craig
     FFA 5-87 R. McGown, Larry Jennings
8. **Walk on Water** FA 6-87 R. McGown, W. Wallace
9. **Mind Games** FFA 5-26-87 R. McGown, T. Olson
10. **Wizard** FA 5-26-87 R. McGown, T. Olson, D. Wright

Far East Wall
1. **Great Wall of China** GFA 4-87 R. McGown and partner
2. **High Road to China** FFA 4-87 R. McGown, W. Wallace
3. **Chinese Finger Torture** GFA 4-87 R. McGown, T. Simms
4. **The Wanderer** FFA 9-87 D. Wright
5. **Ghost Rider** FFA 6-87 R. McGown, T. Olson, D. Wright
6. **Flight of the Seventh Moon** FFA 5-87 M. Pajunas
7. **Orient Express** FFA 5-87 M. Pajunas, Rita Hansen, Charlie Martin, G. Rall
8. **Secret Maze** FFA 6-87 M. Pajunas, R. McGown, D. Wright
9. **Tigers Eye** FFA 4-9-88 T. Olson, G. Lyon, Matt Papolski, Mike Larsen

Warrior Wall
1. **Smears For Fears** FFA 8-85 M. Pajunas, J. Parsley
2.
3. **Crack Warrior** FFA 8-85 M. Pajunas, J. Parsley
4. **You'll Dance to Anything** (TR) 7-88 G. Lyon
5. **Shear Madness** FFA 7-87 M. Pajunas, J. McCracken
6. **Quarry Cracker** FA 1986 M. Pajunas
7. **Lathe of Heaven** FA 1989 R. McGown and partner

8. **Arch Nemesis** FFA 8-85 R. McGown, D. Nakahira
9. **Boy Sage** FA 5-87 R. McGown, Roger Baker
10. **Jealous Rage** FA 5-87 R. McGown, R. Baker
11. **Emotional Rescue** GFFA 9-85 M. Pajunas, J. Parsley

Freeway Wall
1. **Simple Twist** GFA 4-87 R. McGown, C. McMullin, J. Fredericks
2. **Hyper Twist** FFA 5-87 D. Wright
3. **Passing Lane** GFA 5-87 M. Pajunas
4. **Speeding Down South** FA 5-87 M. Pajunas
5. **Ranger Danger** FFA 5-22-87 R. McGown, T. Olson
6. **Telegraph Road** (TR) 5-87 D. Wright
7. **Highway Star** GFA 7-77 Doug Bower, Shari Kearney, R. McGown
8. **Dead Mans Curve** FFA 5-87 R. McGown, T. Olson

Mean Street
1. **Thunder Road** GFFA 4-87 R. McGown, Jim Opdycke
2. **Lethal Ethics** FFA 6-87 W. Wallace, Dave Bloom
3. **Spiritual Journey** FFA 4-87 W. Wallace, R. McGown
4. **Little Arete** FFA 6-87 R. McGown, W. Wallace
5. **Seamingly Endless** FFA 4-87 R. McGown, W. Wallace
6. **Holy Bubbles** GFA 1983 G. Rall
   FFA
7. **Pluto** FA Summer 1990 C. Franklin
8. **Stump the Jock** FA
⊗. **Packin' Heat** FA 8-28-93 D. Sowerby
10. **No Leverage** FA 4-87 Mark Kerns
11. **Be Bold Or Not To Be** = True Blue Water Course
12. **Claymation** FFA 4-87 R. McGown, W. Wallace

Easy Street
xx Short Climbs

Toothpick Wall
1. **Reach For The Sky** GFA 4-87 M. Pajunas, G. Rall
2. **Zenith** (TR) 7-88 G. Lyon, Matt Pixler
3. **Blueberry Jam** FA 1977 R. McGown, Mike Smelsar
⊗. **Joy Ride** FFA 4-24-94 Mike Boehlke, Josh Dearing
4. **Leading Edge** FA 4-87 R. McGown, W. Wallace
5. **Close To The Edge** FA (FFA?) 7-77 R. McGown, Doug Bower
6. **Toothpick** FA 1978 R. McGown, J. Sprecher
7. **Far From The Edge** (TR)
8. **Rob's Ravine** FA 1978 Bill Antel, R. McGown
9. **Competitive Edge** GFA 4-87 R. McGown, W. Wallace, D. Nakahira, C. Carlson

10. **Vertical Therapy** FA 1986 J. Parsley, Dennis Hemminger
11. **Power Surge** FFA 4-87 W. Wallace, R. McGown
12. **Stiff Fingers** FA 1986 D. Hemminger

Boulders In The Woods
xx

Breakfast Cracks
1. **"D" and Rising** FA 8-87 R. McGown, J. Mohel
2. **The Arete** FA Summer 1991 C. Franklin
3. **Blackberry Jam** FRA 1974 Jim Davis, T. Crossman
    FFA 1977 R. McGown, M. Smelsar
4. **Hot Tang** FA 1978 Ted Johnson, R. McGown, F. Ziel
5. **Expresso** FA 1977 Mark Simpson, Rich Warren, Scott Woolums
6. **Red Zinger** FA 7-87 R. McGown, D. Wright
7. **Orange Spice** FA 5-87 R. McGown, T. Olson, Dave Sagient
8. **Lemon Twist** FFA 5-87 R. McGown, T. Olson, D. Sagient
9. **Lunge and Plunge** (TR) Bill Coe, Mike Kruger
10. **White Rabbit** FRA 1977 R. McGown, M. Smelsar
11. **White Rabbit Buttress** (TR) 1984 D. Nakahira, B. Casey
    FFA Unknown
12.
13.
14. **Bird of Paradise** FA 1979 D. Bower, R. McGown, R. Baker
15.
16. **Wisdom Tooth** FA 1978 R. McGown, T. Yates, J. Alzner
17.
18. **Trix are for Kids** (TR)
19. **Time of Your Life** (TR)
20. **Swiss Miss** FA Unknown

Wall of Shadows
1. **Shadows in Space** FA 1986 R. McGown, M. Simpson
2. **Face Disgrace** (variation) FA 1986 R. McGown, M. Simpson
3. **Skywalker** GFA 1986 R. McGown, M. Simpson
4. **Mystic Traveler** FA 7-85 M. Pajunas
    FFA (?) R. McGown, M. Simpson
5. **Spiderline** GFA 1986 R. McGown, M. Simpson
6. **Foot Loose** FA 5-85 M. Pajunas, J. Parsley
7. **Joe's Garden** FA 6-85 J. Parsley, M. Pajunas
8. **Hang Loose** FFA 10-15-88 W. Wallace
9. **Seventh Wave** FA (?) M. Pajunas

CARVER BRIDGE CLIFF

Rockgarden Wall

1. **Crack in the Mirror** FFA 9-21-87 Mike Pajunas
2. **Unknown** FA Unknown
3. **Notorious** FA 9-22-87 M. Pajunas, R. McGown, Gary Rall
   FFA 10-87 M. Pajunas, Darryl Nakahira
4. **Margueritaville** GFFA Fall 1987 R. McGown, D. Nakahira
5. **Cherry Cola** FFA 8-89 G. Rall
6. **Uncola** FA 9-30-87 Tim Olson, R. McGown
   FFA Unknown
7. **Neptune** FA 9-87 T. Olson, R. McGown
8. **Smooth Torquer** FFA 5-89 Greg Lyon
9. **Smerk** FA 1st pitch 9-7-87 T. Olson, R. McGown
   FFA complete 10-15-88 T. Olson, Cecil Colley
10. **New Generation** FFA 1st pitch 8-23-87 Chris McMullin, T. Olson
    FFA complete 2-88 T. Olson, R. McGown, G. Lyon
11. **Free Ride** FFA 6-89 G. Lyon
12. **Scotch and Soda** FFA 9-7-87 T. Olson, R. McGown
13. **Tequila Sunrise** FFA 1st pitch 9-87 R. McGown, T. Olson
    FFA complete 2-88 T. Olson, G. Lyon
14. **Red Dihedral** FA Unknown
    FFA 6-11-88 T. Olson, Matt Pixler
15. **Unknown** (TR)
16. **Jungle Safari** FFA (complete) 3-88 W. Wallace, T. Olson
17. **Night Vision** FA 11-8-87 T. Olson, G. Lyon
    FFA complete 2-88 T. Olson, W. Wallace
18. **Sanity Assassin** FFA 11-87 G. Lyon, T. Olson
19. **Sea of Holes** FA 10-11-87 T. Olson, G. Lyon
    FFA complete 7-21-89 W. Wallace, T. Olson
⊗. **Sport Court** FFA Spring 1990 G. Lyon
20. **Shadow Fox** FFA 10-11-87 T. Olson, G. Lyon
21. **Battleship Arete** FFA 8-89 Virgil Morresette, T. Olson
22. **Night Life** FFA 8-89 T. Olson, V. Morresette
23. **Holiday in Cambodia** (TR) 3-88 W. Wallace
24. **Wally Street** FA 6-21-88 Bruce Casey
25. **Wally Wedding** FFA 10-25-88 D. Nakahira
26. **Sweat and the Flies** FFA 9-18-88 T. Olson

Wall In Between

1. **Passport to Insanity** FFA 3-88 T. Olson, G. Lyon, W. Wallace
2. **Burning From The Inside** FFA 5-88 G. Lyon
3. **Hinge of Fate** FFA 3-88 T. Olson, G. Lyon, R. McGown
4. **Eyes of a Stranger** FFA 4-16-88 T. Olson
5. **Shady Personality** FFA 3-88 T. Olson, G. Lyon, W. Wallace
6. **Rats in the Jungle** FFA 6-26-88 T. Olson, Matt Papolski

Yellow Wall

1. **Call to Greatness** GFA and FFA 2-88 W. Wallace, T. Olson
2. **Plastic Monkey** FFA 11-89 G. Rall
3. **Rites of Passage** FFA 1-88 T. Olson, R. McGown
   FFA complete D. Nakahira and partner
4. **Digital** FFA 5-25-89 G. Lyon
5. **Angular Motion** GFA 1975 Jeff Alzner, Terry Jenkins
   FFA 4-27-88 G. Lyon
6. **Out on a Limb** FFA 12-87 T. Olson, R. McGown, G. Lyon
7. **Smooth Operator** FA Unknown
8. **Talent Show** FA Unknown
9. **Blue Monday** FA Unknown
10. **Crimson Tide** FRA Summer 1976 Mark Simpson, Doug McMillan
11. **Spearfishing in Bermuda** FRA Summer 1976 M. Simpson, D. McMillan
12. **Leaning Uncertainty** FA Unknown
13. **King Rat** FFA 7-7-88 T. Olson, Mike Larson
14. **Chariots of Fire** GFA 2-88 W. Wallace, R. McGown
    FFA 7-6-89 W. Wallace or Blake Hankins

Ivy League Buttress

1. **Dreamscape** GFFA Winter 1988 R. McGown, G. Lyon, T. Olson
2. **Rip Grip** FFA 6-13-88 G. Lyon
3. **Rubicon** FFA 2-88 T. Olson, G. Lyon
4. **Edge of the Reef** FFA complete 3-14-89 T. Olson, G. Lyon
5. **Great Barrier Reef** FA 1-88 W. Wallace
6. **Penguins in Heat** FFA 5-2-90 Jay Green and partner
7. **Challenger** FFA 4-88 W. Wallace, G. Lyon
8. **Last of the Mohicans** FFA 8-19-88 T. Olson
9. **Riders of the Purple Sage** FFA 1st pitch 8-21-88 T. Olson, Cecil Colley
   FA 2nd pitch 8-88 T. Olson, R. McGown

BEACON ROCK

1. **Pacific Rim** FFA 9-10-89 Wayne Wallace, Tim Olson
2. **Boardwalk** FFA Fall 1985 Bill Coe, Bob McMahon
3.
4.
5. **Obnoxious Cubbyhole** GFA 1977 Dick Morse, Chet Sutterlin
6. **Stone Rodeo** FA 5-87 W. Wallace, Robert McGown
   FFA 6-87 R. McGown, Dan Wright
7. **Rock Police** FFA 9-11-89 W. Wallace, R. McGown
8. **Return to the Sky** GFA 7-84 R. McGown, Mark Simpson
9. **Sky Pilot** GFA 4-85 R. McGown, Scott Woolums
10. **Couchmaster** GFA 1985 Bill Coe, Gary Rall, Jim Opdycke

11. **Jingus Jam** FA 4-85 S. Woolums, R. McGown
12. **Cruisin' Direct Finish** FA 1-6-87 R. McGown, W. Wallace
13. **Cosmic Dust** FA 1985 R. McGown, S. Woolums
    FFA ? Darryl Nakahira
14. **Cruisin'** FA 1985 Dennis Hemminger, J. Opdycke
15. **Stardust** FA 1985 Scott Tracy, J. Opdycke
16. **Rock Master** FA 1985 B. Coe, J. Opdycke, Gini Hornbecker
    FFA 1985 Bruce Casey and partner
17. **Rookie Nookie** FA 1985 S. Woolums, R. McGown
       FFA 1986 S. Tracy, J. Opdycke
18. **Icy Treats** FFA 12-84 Mark Cartier, D. Nakahira
19. **Switchblade** GFA 3-85 R. McGown, Guigi Regis
20. **Bladerunner** GFA 3-85 R. McGown, G. Regis
    FFA 7-14-86 Jeff Thomas
21. **Fire and Ice** FFA 6-30-90 T. Olson, Jim Yoder
22. **More Balls Than Nuts** FFA Spring 1985 M. Cartier, D. Nakahira
23. **No Balls No Falls** FFA Spring 1986 S. Tracy, J. Opdycke
24. **Levitation Blues** GFA 1985 J. Yoder, R. McGown, J. Opdycke
25. **Repo Man** FA Summer 1985 (?) R. McGown, M. Simpson
26. **Cigarette** FFA 3-1-87 T. Olson
27. **Lethal Ejection** FA 1985 Ron Allen, J. Opdycke
28. **South East Face** GFA 4-29-54 John Ohrenschall, Gene Todd
29. **Variation** FA 1974 Steve Lyford and partner
30. **Desdichado (var.)** FFA 10-89 W. Wallace, T. Olson
31. **Dyna Flux** FA 10-89 R. McGown and partner
32.
33. **Jill's Thrill** GFA 1985 R. McGown, J. Opdycke, Jill Green
34. **Tooth Faerie** FFA 7-26-92 T. and Cindy Olson
35. **To The Edge And Beyond** FFA 8-88 W. Wallace, Reinhold Buche
36. **Fear of Flying** GFA 1985 R. McGown, Guigi Regis
37. **Desperado** FA 1975 R. McGown, J. Opdycke
38. **Right Gull** GFA 1965 Dean Caldwell, Chuck Brown
    FFA 10-72 Dean Fry
39. **Vulcans Variation** FFA 9-86 T. Olson
40. **Muriel's Memoir** FFA 7-77 Muriel Lodder (Sharp), R. McGown
41. **Synapse** FFA 8-90 R. McGown, W. Wallace
42. **Death and Taxes** FFA 8-2-90 W. Wallace
43. **Lost Variation** GFA 5-10-58 Charlie Carpenter, Paul Resta
44. **Elusive Element** FFA 6-22-90 R. McGown, W. Wallace
45. **Cloud Nine** FFA 10-24-87 W. Wallace, T. Olson
46. **High and Mighty** FA 6-5-89 W. Wallace, T. Olson
47. **Sacrilege** FFA 9-18-90 T. Olson
48.
49. **Diagonal Desperation** FA 1978 R. McGown, S. Woolums
50.

51. **Riverside** FA 10-13-77 J. Thomas, Jim Dunavant
52.
53.
54. **Little Wing** FFA 1985 J. Opdycke, R. McGown, M. Cartier
    FA 2nd-3rd pitch R. McGown, S. Tracy
55. **Broken Arrow** FA 1975 R. McGown, J. Green
56. **Idiot** FA 1985 R. McGown
    FFA Summer 1985 M. Cartier
57. **Magic Fingers** FA 1985 J. Yoder, R. McGown, J. Opdycke
58. **Wrong Gull** FA 1977 (?) Avery Tichner
    FFA 8-31-77 J. Thomas, Shari Kearney, Jack Holmgren
59. **Sorceror's Apprentice** FA 1980 R. McGown, Jim Olson
60. **Old Warriors Never Die** FFA 1990 Jim Yoder
61. **Seagull** GFA 1st pitch 9-3-77 R. McGown, J. Thomas
    (1st pitch also known as **Ten-A-Cee Stemming** with a
    FFA in 1979 by A. Tichner)
    FA complete 10-4-77 J. Thomas, J. Dunavant
62. **Av's Route** FFA 1979 A. Tichner
63. **Too Close for Comfort** FFA 8-27-88 W. Wallace, R. Buche
64. **Left Gull** GFA 1965 D. Caldwell, C. Erwin
    FRFA 7-6-73 J. Thomas, Steve Lyford
65. **Summer Daze** GFA 1975 (?) A. Tichner, R. McGown
    FFA Spring 1985 M. Cartier, D. Nakahira
66.
67. **Bluebird Direct** FA 10-16-77 J. Thomas, B. Casey
68. **Spring Fever** FA Spring 1986 S. Tracy, J. Opdycke
69. **Winter Delight** FFA 1988 R. Allen, Mike Jackson
70. **Sufficiently Breathless** FA Summer 1977 S. Woolums, Terry Yates,
    R. McGown
71. **Fall Guy** FFA Fall 1990 R. Allen, S. Tracy
72. **Aging Fags** FFA Summer 1985 A. Tichner
73. **Blownout Direct** FFA Fall 1990 S. Tracy, J. Opdycke
74. **Tombstone Territory** FA Fall 1990 J. Opdycke, M. Simpson
75. **Bluebird** GFA 1972 Jeff Elphinston, Dave Mention
    FFA 9-11-76 J. Thomas, Monty Mayko, Ed Newville
76. **Variation** FA (original finish) 1972 J. Elphinston, D. Mention
77. **Bridge of the Gods** GFA 1987 R. McGown, W. Wallace, S. Woolums
    FFA
78. **Pirates** FA R. McGown
    FFA July 1985 M. Cartier, D. Nakahira
79. **Blownout** GFA 1-19/20-69 Steve Strauch, Danny Gates
    FFA 10-16-76 J. Thomas, Ken Currens
80. **Second Wind** FA Fall 1981 Ted Johnson, Bill Strayer
81. **Borderline** FFA 1st pitch 6-1-89 T. Olson, Tim Wolfe, Neal Olson

FFA 2nd pitch 6-4-89 T. Olson, W. Wallace
82. **Grunge Book** GFA 5-70 Wayne Haack, Steve Strauch
83. **Excalibur** FFA 7-8-90 T. Olson, W. Wallace
84. **Crankenstein**
85. **Wild Turkeys** FA Summer 1970 Brian Holcomb, Neal Olson, Glen Kirkpatrick
86.
87. **Psychic Wound** FFA Spring 1985 S. Tracy, J. Opdycke
88. **Flying Dutchman** GFA Fall 1984 Bob McMahon, J. Opdycke, B. Coe
FFA Fall 1984 M. Cartier
89. **Bears in Heat** FFA Summer 1985 M. Cartier, D. Nakahira
90. **Dirty Double Overhang** GFA 7-73 Alan Kearney, Dave Henry, Malcolm Ulrich
91. **Smooth Dancer** GFA Summer 1974 A. Kearney, Les Nugent, M. Ulrich
92.
93. **Takes Fist** GFA Spring 1981 T. Johnson, Mike Pajunas
FFA 6-29-81 M. Cartier, J. Thomas
94.
95. **Ground Zero** GFA Summer 1984 J. Opdycke, B. Coe, Jay Bergren
FFA 1985 D. Nakahira, M. Cartier
96. **Nuke-U-Later** FFA 1987 (?) R. Allen, and partner
97. **Iron Maiden** GFA 3-85 R. McGown, Jeff Alzner
98. **Flying Swallow** GFA 1965 Kim Schmitz, Earl Levin, D. Caldwell
FFA 8-10-77 J. Thomas, Del Young
99. **Variation** FA 8-10-77 J. Thomas, M. Cartier
100. **Direct Start (to Flying Swallow)** TR
101. **Local Access Only** FFA 8-89 Nathan Charleton, Eric Freden
102. **Reasonable Richard** FFA 9-89 T. Olson, N. Olson, Jim Davis
103. **Black Maria** FFA 9-23-89 T. Olson, E. Freden, N. Charleton, Tim Doyle
104. **Flight Time** FA 1st pitch 7-77 J. Thomas, M. Cartier
FFA 1st pitch 8-1-81 J. Thomas, M. Cartier
FFA 2nd pitch 1984 J. Olson
FA 3rd pitch 1977 R. McGown, B. Antel
105.
106. **Flying Circus** FA 1st pitch 6-18-77 J. Thomas, N. Olson
FA complete J. Thomas, Mike Smelsar
107. **Blood, Sweat and Smears** FA 7-20-77 J. Thomas, R. McGown
108. **True Grunt** FA 7-77 J. Thomas, M. Cartier
109. **Steppenwolf** GFA 5-71 Les Nugent, Bill Herman, Bill Nickle
FFA (to Big Ledge) 5-77 R. McGown, Levi Grey
FA (above Big Ledge) 7-78 R. McGown, Doug Bower
FFA (above Big Ledge for 80') 1982 or 83 Alan Lester, M. Cartier
110. **Dod's Jam** GFA (to Big Ledge) Summer 1961 Eugene Dod, Bob Martin, E. Levin

The first ascent may have been via a direct line like Free For All
FA complete 5-72 J. Thomas, Dean Fry
FFA Summer 1972 Wayne Arrington, Jack Barrar
FA Osprey Variation 1972 by Jack Barrar and Wayne Arrington

111. **Dod's Deviation** FA 6-12-77 R. McGown, M. Smelsar
112. **Journey to the East** GFA Spring 1983 R. McGown
113. **Devil's Backbone** FA 1989 N. Charleton, R. Allen
114. **The Norseman** FFA 7-14-88 M. Cartier
115. **Dastardly Crack** FA 1965 B. Martin, K. Schmitz, Gerald Bjorkman
     FFA 7-6-73 J. Thomas, Steve Lyford
116. **Squeeze Box** FA 7-20-77 R. McGown, J. Thomas
117. **Edge of Fear** GFA 6-89 R. McGown, Steve Hillinger
118. **Free For All** FA 8-73   D. Fry, S. Lyford
119. **Free For Some** FA Unknown
     FRA Summer 1977 R. McGown, M. Smelsar
120. **Windsurfer** FA 9-86 R. McGown, S. Woolums
121. **Fresh Squeeze** FA Summer 1989 N. Charleton, E. Freden
122.
123. **Pipeline** GFA Summer 1977 R. McGown
     FFA 8-2-81 T. Johnson, Charlie Priest
124. **Pipe Dream** GFA 5-84 R. McGown, B. Antel
     FFA 7-84 J. Olson, M. Dennuci
125. **Pipeline Headwall** FFA 5-85 R. McGown, B. Antel
126. **Silver Crow** GFA 5-82 R. McGown, M. Simpson
127. **Axe of Karma** GFA 4-86 R. McGown, Bob Scarborough
128. **Red Ice** GFFA 2-86 R. McGown, S. Woolums
129. **Doubting Thomas** FA Unknown
130. **Boys of Summer** FFA 5-86 R. McGown, M. Simpson
131. **Fingers of a Fisherman** GFFA 5-86 R. McGown, R. Krukowski
132. **Crack of Dawn** GFA 1986 R. McGown, R, Krukowski
133. **Jensen's Ridge** GFA 1968 B. Martin, D. Jensen
     FFA 4-13-74 J. Thomas
134. **Updraft to Heaven** GFA 6-77 R. McGown, L. Grey
135. **Mostly Air** GFA Summer 1981 R. McGown, M. Simpson
136. **Lay Lady Lay** FA 6-77 R. McGown, M. Simpson
137. **Rip City** FA 7-9-77 J. Thomas, M. Smelsar
138. **Hard Times** FA 7-3-77 J. Thomas
139. **Ragtime** FA 11-12-76 J. Thomas, Willis Krause
     FFA 1981 T. Johnson, D. Young
140. **Synchronicity** FA Summer 1982 R. McGown, J. Olson
141. **Boulder Problem in the Sky** FA 4-7-74 J. Thomas, Tim Miller
     FFA 11-11-76 J. Thomas, C. Sutterlin
142. **Iron Cross** GFA 7-8-77 R. McGown, M. Lodder
143. **Variation** FA 10-22-76 D. Young, J. Thomas

Index